"I

Remember

When..."

Policing in the Thames Valley – then and now

By
Tony Keep

© Anthony R Keep

First published 2012 by Anthony Keep

ISBN   978-0-9572702-0-6

All monies raised by the sale of this book will be donated to The Police Rehabilitation Trust and Flint House, the Police Rehabilitation Centre at Goring, Oxfordshire.

Printed and bound in Great Britain by Oxuniprint
(The printing division of Oxford University Press).

CONTENTS

Memories of:

CONTENTS

CONTENTS

CONTENTS

FOREWORD

Change affects us all, and this is perhaps no more evident than in the police service. Politics, technology and the economy never stand still, and their impact on modern policing is significant. Keeping up with this change can be both challenging and exciting, so it is interesting to read about and reflect upon many of the memories documented in this book.

The approach Tony has taken in "I Remember When..." provides a real personal insight into a number of changes we have all experienced over the years, many of which happened before I myself joined the service, and many others that have occurred during my career. Whether a serving or retired police officer, someone with a connection to policing, or someone with no connection at all, this book is fascinating, providing us with accurate reflections on a very important part of social history.

As a serving police officer, I have been left wondering how on earth we managed to provide the high quality service we did without modern technology and techniques, as well as contemplating what further changes to policing tomorrow might bring!

I am delighted that the money raised from the sale of this book is to be donated to The Police Rehabilitation Trust and Flint House Rehabilitation Centre. Both of these registered charities provide much needed care and support to sick and injured police officers (both serving and retired), and both charities rely on donations and subscription from serving officers.

I hope many people take the opportunity to read the book and learn or reflect upon the development of policing over the years, while also providing a valuable contribution to these worthwhile police charities.

Sara Thornton CBE, QPM

Chief Constable
Thames Valley Police

Thames Valley Constabulary helmet plate

Thames Valley Police helmet plate

PREFACE

The idea for 'I Remember When…' came when I was talking to a fellow retired police officer about a procedure that took place in the police force he joined (Reading Borough), and I realised that these individual memories would be lost when people passed on.

Social history is popular today, especially with people researching family trees. I therefore felt that people may be interested in the policies, procedures and processes that were followed, in years gone by, in the police forces that made up the Thames Valley Police area. Many of these policies, and procedures may seem completely out of place in today's modern, technological, statistically accountable police service.

I served in the Berkshire Constabulary as a police cadet from 1963 to 1966, then as a police constable. In April 1968, Berkshire Constabulary amalgamated with the surrounding county forces of Buckinghamshire and Oxfordshire and with the urban forces of Oxford City and Reading Borough, to become the Thames Valley Constabulary (later renamed the Thames Valley Police).

I am grateful to members of the Berkshire, Buckinghamshire, and Oxfordshire branches of the National Association of Retired Police Officers *(NARPO)* for their individual contribution of their memories that have supported mine in the contents of this book. These memories mainly cover the period from the 1950s through to the early 1990s. The earliest memories come from an officer who initially joined in January 1940.

Please remember that these are memories, and memories can change over time. Where the source of the memory is from more than one person, details have been included. I therefore apologise if some of the memories are not factually accurate, or not as you may remember them.

In addition to the aim of recording the memories, this book is also produced to raise money for the Police Rehabilitation Trust and in particular the Police Rehabilitation Centre at Flint House, Goring. All the profits from the sale will be donated to the Police Rehabilitation Trust and Flint House. More information on the Trust and Flint House is given on page 11.

The book is divided into sections and sub-sections to enable readers, if they so wish, to research particular subjects. Some memories may appear under more than one section. However, as general enjoyment, the book can be read from cover to cover.

Each section will describe various policies, procedures and processes from the past, and will give an overall summary of present policies, procedures and processes. No comment is made to compare past with present, as without change where would we be? The only comment I make is what would the contents of this book be in 2050, looking back to policing now?

Should you have a memory that you feel could have been included in 'I Remember When…', please forward it to tonykeep@btinternet.com, and if sufficient are received I will produce an additional edition of this book to raise further funds for the Police Rehabilitation Trust. Should you feel that the format of the booklet could be used for other force areas or services, please remember that this booklet has not been produced for personal gain, but to raise money for charity and in particular Flint House.

Depending upon your age and background you may view the contents of this booklet with nostalgia or with humour. I hope you enjoy reading it.

If you would like to know more about today's Thames Valley Police, go to www.thamesvalley.police.uk

Anthony R. Keep (Tony)
(Retired: Reading 1995)

Police Rehabilitation Trust and Flint House

Police Rehabilitation Centre, Flint House

Founded in 1890 by Miss Catherine Gurney OBE and based in Hove, West Brighton until the Centre moved to its present location in South Oxfordshire in 1988, the Police Rehabilitation Centre Flint House provides high standards of individually planned intensive rehabilitation and convalescent programmes for sick and injured serving and retired police officers.

The Centre offers a holistic environment for the undertaking of intensive rehabilitation, physiotherapy, general nursing, psychological support, and drug and alcohol counselling, supported with complementary treatments including health promotion, acupuncture, aromatherapy, pilates, and comprehensive fitness and leisure facilities.

Serving donating officers normally undertake a free of charge 12-day stay (retired officers 7 days) in order to facilitate effective and individual treatment programmes.

Admissions are normally administered at Force level by the Occupational Health or Welfare departments in conjunction with the local Federation JBB. In most cases, attendance at Flint House is classed as special duty time thus officers are not taking annual leave or sick leave to come to the Centre.

More than 3000 officers are admitted annually.

The main income of the Centre derives from a small weekly charitable donation made by serving officers within the 29 forces covered by the Centre. No regular central Government or local authority funding is received.

Acknowledged with an 'Excellence' rating by the Care Quality Commission, Flint House is highly regarded by officers who have experienced the Centre's environment and is consistently credited with assisting in the return of officers to full duties earlier than expected.

More information, admission criteria, news, updates and video footage is available at www.flinthouse.co.uk. There is also a dedicated Facebook page.

Police Rehabilitation Centre,
Flint House, Reading Road,
Goring-on-Thames,
Oxfordshire, RG8 0LL
T: 01491 874499
enquiries@flinthouse.co.uk
www.flinthouse.co.uk

ACKNOWLEDGEMENTS

This book would not have been possible without the memories provided by members of the Berkshire, Buckinghamshire and Oxfordshire branches of the National Association of Retired Police Officers *(NARPO)*, and I thank them for their contributions.

In my research to compare past with present, I took advantage of the 'Ride Along' scheme at Thames Valley Police which enables civilians to observe police officers in the operational environment.

I experienced late shifts at Reading, Loddon Valley and Roads Policing, Taplow, and would like to thank the following officers for their patience in having 'one of the old boys along'.

Reading: Inspector Mick Osbourne and his team, in particular Constables Scott Whelan and Barry Gould. Loddon Valley: Inspector Warren McKeown and his team, in particular Acting Sergeant Phil Davies and Constable Tim Cameron. Taplow: Sergeant Carl Kneale and 'A' Shift, in particular Constable Chris Howlett.

I visited the Windsor Police Enquiry Centre *(PEC)*, and would like to thank Julian Heard and Sarah Jarman for their help and guidance and their demonstration of the technical systems available to them in providing response to the public.

I also visited Abingdon Control Room and would like to thank Inspector Jim Biscoe, the Abingdon Control Room Manager for arranging the visit and demonstration of the systems available in the Control Room, especially the radio and mapping systems.

My experience from the 'Ride alongs' and the visit to the PEC and Control Room left me with the view that apart from the increase in overall workload, the personal interaction with the public when out of the car has not changed. What has changed is the technology supporting that interaction, and the recording necessities prior to and from that interaction, brought about by the accountability and statistics monitoring requirement placed on today's police service.

I also thank Sergeant Rob Murray, now Inspector Rob Murray for his general information of current day practices and Inspector Chris Ward, Foundation Training Manager for his information and advice re current training policies and procedures of new police officers.

Lastly I wish to thank Shelagh Leonard, Force-wide Internal Communications and Change Manager, Thames Valley Police and her team especially: Jonathan Hall, Publication Officer, for his assistance and advice, in particular his painstaking and thorough proof reading; Steve Smith, Graphic Designer for his assistance and advice re graphics and printing, and Ken Wells, Thames Valley Force Museum Curator for identification and provision of some of the photographs used.

COMMUNICATION

Communication, whether oral or visual, is probably the area of most change and advancement over the years.

Listed below are some of the memories of retired officers and an indication of the changes that have occurred as a result of technology.

Telephones

I Remember When…

Memory of:
Maurice Hedges *(Joined Berkshire as a junior clerk in 1940 - forerunner of police cadets - appointed after national service, a constable in 1946, retired in 1975 from Wokingham).*

Maurice remembers, on joining as a junior clerk, working in the Telephone Room, part of the Telephone and Communication Section in the Berkshire Constabulary Headquarters which was, at that time, based in Reading. Maurice describes the room as the nerve centre of the Berkshire Constabulary. The Telephone Room was in the charge of a police constable, assisted by a civilian senior clerk, and junior clerks. A switchboard connected the six divisions of the Berkshire force and Reading Borough Police Force, plus internal extensions within the Berkshire Headquarters. There were five General Post Office *(GPO)* lines, one of which was used for 'Air Raid Warnings' and another as a direct line to Berkshire County Council.

I Remember When…

Memory of:
Personal memory.

When I first joined Berkshire Constabulary, as a cadet in 1963, I was posted to the Force Control Room at Sulhamstead, the Headquarters of the Berkshire Constabulary.

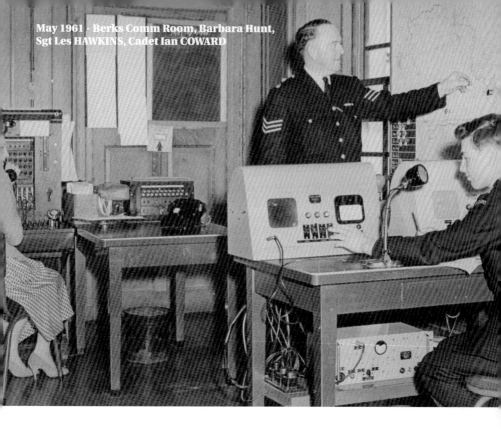

May 1961 - Berks Comm Room, Barbara Hunt, Sgt Les HAWKINS, Cadet Ian COWARD

At this time the telephone systems within the Headquarters and the main stations were all manual. If automatic telephone systems had been invented, they had not reached the Berkshire Constabulary. This meant that when a person in an office wished to contact another office within the Headquarters, or a divisional station, they had to lift the office telephone and wait for the switchboard operator in the Control Room to answer. The switchboard operator picked up a cord and plugged it into the extension that was calling, then picked up the matching cord and plugged it into the extension the caller required, and manually rang the extension.

If the person calling required an outside telephone number, the switchboard operator had to connect the matching cord to an outside line, dial the number and wait for the number to answer.

If the caller at Headquarters wanted a person at a divisional station, the caller had to be first answered by the switchboard operator in the Headquarters Control Room, who would connect them to the switchboard operator at the divisional headquarters, who had to manually ring the extension in the divisional headquarters – *It took time!*

COMMUNICATION

What happens now…

It is difficult to imagine a telephone system where all calls had to go through a switchboard. Today, all telephones both at work and at home are automatic dialing systems and, of course, there are mobile phones. Effectively there are two telephone numbers for Thames Valley Police.

The emergency number is 999. For all non emergency calls 101 is used. Thames Valley Police joined the national single non-emergency number scheme on 14th November 2011.

In addition to the above there is a direct dial system where the STD code for the area, a two digit pre number and the extension number of the person to be called, are used. Direct dial numbers are quoted in all Thames Valley communications.

Police officers are issued with a mobile phone, a personal radio and all police officers and civilian employees have a Thames Valley Police email address and an access password into the Force computer system to access emails. All three systems can be used to contact the officer, and voicemail messages can be left on the officer's mobile phone.

I Remember When…

Memory of:
Personal memory.

All private telephone calls had to be paid for. As all calls had to be dialled by the switchboard operator, persons requesting the call had to stipulate if it was a private call. In these cases the number was logged and timed. If it was a long distance call that had to be made through the exchange operator, the switchboard operator when requesting the number would have to ask for an 'ADC' call. This was 'advise duration and charge'. At the conclusion of the call, the exchange would telephone the switchboard operator and inform them of the time and cost of the call. This was logged.

At the end of the month, the daytime civilian switchboard operator would send out accounts to all people who had made private calls, and these were paid into the Administration Department.

What happens now...

Most people will have access to their own mobile phone. Private calls, using the Force telephone system should not be made unless it relates to a welfare issue e.g. explaining that a person will be late off duty.

Teleprinters

I Remember When...

Memory of:
Maurice Hedges *(Joined Berkshire as a junior clerk in 1940 - forerunner of police cadets - appointed after national service, a constable in 1946, retired in 1975 from Wokingham).*

Maurice remembers on joining the Berkshire Constabulary in 1940, a teleprinter system had not then been installed within the Force. All messages received were by telephone and handled by the Telephone Room. The messages were written out in triplicate on telephone message pads (one copy for the department concerned, one copy for the Information Room, and one copy for the file kept in the room).

Transmission of messages to divisions was by a multi link telephone system, through the switchboard. This enabled a message to be dictated and received at several locations at the same time. When dictating the message, the original message had to be endorsed with the time and date it was sent and name of the person receiving the message at each of the divisions that received it.

Maurice remembers that a teleprinter system was installed in late 1941, but it only connected the Divisional Headquarters in Berkshire and Reading Borough. Initially all messages were sent by manually typing at the time of transmission.

Later, a tape machine was introduced which enabled a message to be first typed, and a tape produced, then the tape fed back through the machine and the message was sent at a faster rate. The teleprinter link used the same line as the telephone system and whenever the teleprinter was connected to a division, the telephone could not be used.

COMMUNICATION

I Remember When...

Memories of:
Malcolm Walker *(Joined Berkshire police cadets in 1967, appointed a constable in Thames Valley in 1970, retired in 1999 from Aylesbury Crown Court Liaison)*
Jamie Eves *(Joined Berkshire police cadets in 1965, appointed a constable in 1966, retired in 1997 from Taplow Traffic)*
Personal memory.

Malcolm and **Jamie** remember when they were cadets at the Divisional Headquarters, receiving information through teleprinter messages from the Berkshire Control Room.

I remember that operating the teleprinter system was part of my duties as a police cadet in the Berkshire Control Room. When a teleprinter message was received in the Control Room for onward circulation, a tape was printed out as the message was received, which was then fed into a machine and the message sent to all the Divisional Headquarters.

Messages were received and sent to external forces and locations via the 'Telex' system which used the teleprinter process. It was a process using the public telephone system, and a link was made with another Telex machine by dialling the appropriate number, very similar to making a telephone call, and sending the message.

Where a message originated at the Berkshire Headquarters the operator first had to type the message out and produce a tape. The message was then sent at a reasonably fast speed, using the tape machine.

The teleprinter circuit to Divisions was over the internal telephone lines, and when a teleprinter message was being sent to a Divisional Station no telephone calls could be made to or from that Divisional Station.

When messages had to be forwarded to sub divisional stations and sector stations, this was no problem if the stations had teleprinters, as the same tape system was used at the Divisional Headquarters. The problem occurred with stations without teleprinters, as messages had to be passed by dictation from one station to the other, a task clearly remembered by **Malcolm** and **Jamie**.

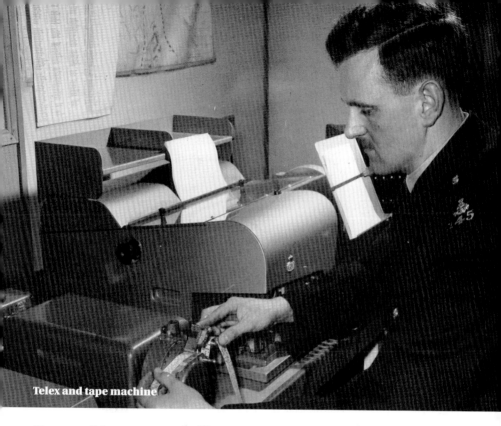

Telex and tape machine

Express Messages and All Ports Warnings

I Remember When…

Memories of:
Maurice Hedges *(Joined Berkshire as a junior clerk in 1940 - forerunner of police cadets - appointed after national service, a constable in 1946, retired in 1975 from Wokingham)*
Dick Godfrey *(Joined Buckinghamshire in 1956, retired in 1986 from Newbury)*
Personal memory.

Maurice remembers the Express Message system when he first joined Berkshire as a Junior Clerk in 1940. When he first joined, a teleprinter system had not been installed so all messages were received by dictation via the telephone and had to be written down on message pads. The Express Message was the heading given to indicate the urgency of the message and speed that circulation was required.

COMMUNICATION

Maurice remembers that all Express Messages had to be written in red ink. Many of the messages related to wanted persons or persons suspected of spying. Messages often originated from New Scotland Yard.

Dick and I both remember the Express Message system. When we joined the Telex and teleprinter systems had been installed. The 'Express Message' heading was given to teleprinter messages indicating the urgency of circulation, either by teleprinter or dictation. The messages would relate to incidents requiring immediate police action, such as a person wanted for a serious crime or an escape of a dangerous prisoner.

Dick remembers that, in Buckinghamshire, details of an Express Message when entered in pocket books had to be in red ink.

I can remember the All Ports Warning message. The sending of an All Ports Warning had to be approved by a Senior Officer. It was a message that required action at exit and entry ports to the UK and was normally related to persons wanted for a serious offence, or possible abduction of a child who may be taken abroad.

The message was initially circulated by Telex to Scotland Yard, who would then send the message to the relevant ports.

What happens now…

With the development of computers came the internet and email. This has replaced Telex and teleprinter messages, and the need for onward circulation of messages by teleprinter or dictation has gone. Message handling is now instantaneous as all messages are sent and received via email. The originator of the message can set the distribution and level of security access for a message. The Force has a central email address, and all officers and civilian employees have their own email addresses. With technology, the speed of delivery has also increased.

COMMUNICATION

Communication before radios

It is difficult, looking at today's ease of access to communication, to understand how a police force was effective without access to radios. However, as will be seen from the memories below, radios in police cars only became operational in 1952 and personal radios were only introduced between 1965 and 1967.

Prior to radios, communication with patrolling police officers was, in the county forces, through telephone boxes, and in the urban forces, by using telephones in specially designed 'Police Boxes' or 'Police Pillars'. This procedure was officially called 'Conference Points' or more normally 'Points'.

Conference Points

I Remember When...

Memories of:
John Harker *(Joined Oxfordshire as a police cadet in 1958, appointed as a constable in 1961, retired in 1987 from Cwmbran District Police Training Centre)*
Personal memory.

John remembers making points at telephone boxes in Oxfordshire. In Oxfordshire the requirement was to wait at each box for 15 minutes, should the station want you. When you were away from the phone box you were uncontactable for 45 minutes of each hour. He remembers at Witney, due to the manual telephone exchange, it was possible for the exchange to ring all phone boxes in a particular area, hoping that the patrolling constable would hear and pick up the phone or a member of the public would pick up the telephone, find the patrolling constable and tell them they were required.

I can remember the points system in Berkshire, when I started at Bracknell in 1966. Points at this time in the Berkshire Force were for ten minutes - you arrived five minutes before the set time and left five minutes after. This meant that as a patrolling officer you were not contactable for 50 minutes out of every hour.

POLICE
FIRE
AMBULANCE
FOR PUBLIC USE

COMMUNICATION

You were unable to contact the police station at any time, unless you carried the necessary pennies to use the telephone or, as often happened, you encouraged the operator to put you through to the police station as you had no change. At this time, most of the telephone exchanges were still local and manual.

All police officers carried whistles as part of their equipment. This was the initial means by which police officers alerted other police officers if they needed assistance. If, however, you were the only officer on patrol in a particular area you had to rely on a member of the public, on hearing a whistle, to phone the police station and inform them of the noise. For the officer needing assistance, they had to hope that the station would then be able to contact an officer, at a point on an adjoining beat, and send them to your assistance. This process obviously took time and there was no confirmation that action had been taken as a result of blowing a whistle, until the assistance arrived.

I Remember When...

Memories of:
Jack Penny *(Joined Reading in 1951, retired in 1983 from Reading, Traffic)*
Geoff Allen *(Joined Reading as a police cadet in 1957, appointed constable in 1959, retired in 1985 from Ascot).*

Jack and **Geoff** both remember the system in Reading Borough where mainly police boxes (which you could go inside – Dr Who had his later) or police pillars were used. The boxes, and some pillars had lights, which could be activated by the station. When they flashed, the patrolling constable was required to answer the phone.

Where your point was at a box or pillar, the patrolling officer had to phone into the station at the required time. There was also a book maintained in the box that had to be signed to confirm the time of visit. Where there was no suitable box or pillar, a telephone box was the nominated point, and the system similar to the county forces used.

COMMUNICATION

I Remember When...

Memory of:
Mike Smith *(Joined Buckinghamshire in 1963, retired in 1993 from Bracknell).*

Mike remembers the police box and pillar system being present and used in High Wycombe when he started there in 1963. The boxes had a light that could be operated from the police station to attract the patrolling constable. Helpful members of the public would often draw the attention of patrolling police officers to a police box if the light was flashing.
(High Wycombe was a Borough Police Force up until 1947, when it was amalgamated into the Buckinghamshire Constabulary).

What happens now...

Points are no longer made as we have an effective personal radio system and mobile phone system that maintains communication with officers at all times.

Problems when not having immediate contact

I Remember When...

Memories of:
Jack Penny *(Joined Reading in 1951, retired in 1983 from Reading, Traffic)*
Geoff Allen *(Joined Reading as a police cadet in 1957, appointed as a constable in 1959, retired in 1985 from Ascot)*
Ian Potter *(Joined Berkshire as a police cadet in 1966, appointed as a constable in 1968, retired in 1997 from Slough).*

Telephone box – only method of contact in rural areas

Jack remembers the problems that occurred when as a patrolling constable you needed to contact the police station.

One late evening he arrested a person for drunk and disorderly in Wokingham Road, Reading, near the Three Tunns Cross Roads, over two miles from the police station. If it had been in the town centre it was normal to walk the prisoner back to the police station, but two miles was too far, especially with a drunk and disorderly person.

A Thames Valley bus was passing enroute to Reading Railway Station, which was near to the police station. Jack stopped the bus and asked if the driver could assist him. The driver was even more helpful than Jack had anticipated - he changed his route as he approached the railway station dropping Jack and his prisoner at Reading Police Station. No fare was required.

Geoff remembers the arrest of one violent drunk in Kings Road, Reading near the junction with Orts Road. It was the policy of Reading Borough not to issue their officers with handcuffs. Arrested people had to be placed in a police hold in order to restrain and move. Unable to summon any assistance, Geoff had to place the man in the required police hold and struggle with him back to the police station. He states he was unable to speak when he arrived there.

Ian remembers a similar situation. In the early hours of the morning he was on a conference point in South Ascot when he received a call from Ascot Police Station about an alarm in a social club in Ascot High Street, some two miles away.

COMMUNICATION

He was on his own and cycled to the club to discover two offenders inside. They ran off, down to the railway line. He had no means to call for other officers to attend - even if he had, there were none immediately available. He gave chase.

One offender left the railway line and went through back gardens, while the other remained on the railway line. Ian gave chase to the offender fleeing over the back gardens and, after several gardens, caught and arrested the offender.

He had no contact with the police station, so handcuffed the arrested person to the garden iron fence, then went back to the railway line and found the second offender, who he arrested.

This one was walked back to Ascot Police Station. Ian's problem was then identifying the back garden of the house where the first offender was handcuffed. After some 20 minutes, the house was identified and the prisoner found, still handcuffed to the fence and waiting to be collected!

What happens now...

With an effective radio system, officers on patrol are able to maintain contact with the control room and keep them updated with their location and needs.
With the arrested drunk in Reading, a van with a cage in the back designed for transporting prisoners would have been sent.
With an alarm activation in the social club, one or more mobile patrolling units would have been sent. As it was in the early hours, each unit would normally be double-crewed.

If a dog handler was available they would have also responded. As the offenders ran off, if the helicopter had been available it would have also attended and the offenders would have been tracked using the helicopter's thermal imaging camera.

With the radio system linked to a mapping system, the control room operator could bring up an enlarged map of the area and when the constable detained the offender in the back garden and radioed in, their call sign would be logged onto the map, giving their exact location and details of the adjoining road and house number. Other units would have been sent to the officer's assistance and to transport the offender back to the police station.

COMMUNICATION

Radio in police vehicles

I Remember When...

Memories of:
Blackney Chambers *(Joined Buckinghamshire in 1950, retired in 1979 from Slough)*
Personal memory.

Blackney remembers that radios were first introduced into various police cars in Buckinghamshire Constabulary in 1952. He had the task of going around the Force, training officers on how to use the radio, with the clear requirement that the full Force call sign of M2HB had to be used, and not shortened to HB. Each vehicle was allocated a number which, when an officer called from the vehicle, had to be prefixed by the Force call sign.

For example, if a call was made from a vehicle to the Control Room it would be 'M2HB30 to M2HB' and this would be replied from the Control Room 'M2HB to M2HB30 pass your message'

I commenced in the Berkshire Constabulary Control Room in 1963, and by this time the M2 had been dropped from the above process, although the official call sign was M2HA.

Buckinghamshire launch new motorcycles, early 1950s - note no radios

MPP 273   MPP 274   MPP 275   MPP 276

JCKS.
JLICE

26

COMMUNICATION

I Remember When…

Memories of:
Geoff Allen *(joined Reading as a police cadet in 1957, appointed as a constable in 1959 retired in 1985 from Ascot)*
John Harker *(joined Oxfordshire as a police cadet in 1958, appointed as a constable in 1961, retired from Cwmbran Police District Training Centre in 1987)*
Personal memory.

Geoff remembers using the car radio system in Reading Borough in 1963. The call sign for the Reading Borough was HT, however the radio system was a joint one with Berkshire Constabulary (call sign HA) and the Berkshire Fire Service (call sign HAF). The system was managed through the Berkshire Control Room, and both Reading Borough and the Berkshire Fire Service had to ask the Berkshire Control Room for access to speak to their vehicles.

John remembers a similar system in Oxfordshire, where the radio channel was controlled by Oxfordshire County Police (call sign HH). Oxford City Police (call sign HR), Oxford County Fire Brigade (call sign HHF), and Oxford City Fire Brigade (call sign HRF) had to ask the control operator in Oxford County Control Room to be connected to speak to their radio vehicles. John can remember that - when connected - all vehicles on the radio scheme could hear what was said from the vehicle. He clearly remembers the transmission from one Oxford County fire appliance that was attending a road traffic accident on the A40 at Wheatley. It went *"Hello HHF, Hello HHF 'Stop' for road traffic accident at Wheatley, it's very foggy, there's going to be another acci…… F…….me, he's hit me up the arse!"*

There would have been a police car already at the first accident to now deal with the second!

I Remember When…

Memory of:
Personal memory.

COMMUNICATION

Following amalgamation in 1968, the Force was split into ten Divisions and three areas covering the radio frequency for vehicles. HB covered "A" Division (Aylesbury), "B" Division (High Wycombe) and "J" Division (Bletchley). HA covered "C" Division (Slough), "D" Division (Bracknell), "E" Division (Reading) and "F" Division (Newbury), with HH covering "G" Division (Banbury) and "H" Division (Oxford). The Traffic Division was split into three areas, based on the radio frequency cover. North East Traffic Area (NETA) covered "A", "B" and "J" Divisions, Southern Traffic Area (STA) covered "C", "D", "E" and "F" Divisions, and North West Traffic Area (NWTA) covered "G" and "H" Divisions.

I can also remember problems that occurred as a result of the limited range of the VHF radio scheme. Radio aerials were positioned on high points throughout the force area and the VHF scheme operated on a 'line of sight' principal. Reception was limited to the distance between the main aerial and the patrolling vehicle and hills that could block the line of sight. Initially the sets in the cars were only set up for the frequency of the force that the car operated in.

Oxford City Wireless Control Room early 1950s

28

COMMUNICATION

Later channel switches were included which enabled the operator in the car to change radio channels (frequencies) as the car moved out of one force radio area into another. If the set was not set up for adjoining frequencies a radio contact was lost when you drove out of the range of your 'home' frequency. This was a problem I sometimes encountered when patrolling the M1 at Newport Pagnell. The traffic cars were equipped with the Bedfordshire force channel, as we operated a joint motorway patrol with them. However if I travelled too far north into Northamptonshire I lost radio contact as the cars were not equipped with the Northamptonshire frequency.

I remember a commitment that required me to travel north, at a fast speed, to liaise with a police vehicle travelling from Yorkshire. Before I left the Thames Valley area, and radio contact, I had to arrange to telephone my control room from Leicestershire Services to get more details.

I then had to stop at Leicester Forest East Services and contact the Thames Valley force control room to be informed that a rendezvous had been arranged for the southbound Trowell Services at Nottingham. At the rendezvous I took over the escort commitment from a West Yorkshire traffic car and returned to the Thames Valley to complete the escort commitment. Due to the radio system, I was out of radio contact for approximately 140 miles of motorway travel.

I Remember When…

Memory of:
Personal memory.

I can remember the obvious benefits that radios in police cars brought to communicating between the police control room and officers in vehicles.

The problem of communication with officers outside of the vehicle still existed. If you remained close to a vehicle, with the radio turned up and the windows down, you could still hear the radio - as could everyone else.

COMMUNICATION

Personal radios

I Remember When...

Memory of:
Personal memory.

I can remember personal radios when they were introduced at Bracknell in 1967. The system was called a Pye Pocket Phone, and consisted of the base station set in the police station, and a two-part set for use outside the police station. The set consisted of the transmitter and receiver. Each was rectangular in shape, measuring approximately two inches wide, by five inches long and one inch thick.

The receiver had a clip on the back which enabled it to be placed inside of your jacket and clipped to the lapel.

The transmitter had a button on the side which, when pushed, projected a four inch aerial from the top of the set. Care had to be taken not to press the button as you closed the set to your mouth to speak, as it was known for the aerial to come out in contact with your nose! There was no carrying harness, so the natural thing was to place the receiver in your pocket.

The issue then was that the button could be pushed against the side of the pocket, the aerial come out and the set start to transmit, unknown to the person carrying it. When a set was transmitting it blocked the system and no other unit or base station could speak.

If you were in a vehicle it was easy to place the transmitter on the dashboard. When you left the vehicle you sometimes forgot to take the transmitter with you - a fact only realised when you were some way from the vehicle and received a call on the receiver which had to be answered, using the transmitter... which was back in the vehicle.

The range for the personal radio scheme was limited in distance and was reduced by tall buildings and hills between the main aerial of the system and the location of the unit. Each police station was equipped with its own scheme, which operated on different frequencies.

With the introduction of personal radios, giving the potential of immediate contact between the patrolling police officer and the station, the need for a conference points patrol system ceased.

COMMUNICATION

I Remember When…

Memory of:
Dave Shillabeer *(Joined Thames Valley in 1971, following military service retired in 1991 from Architectural Liaison, Pangbourne).*

Dave remembers that at Henley, even after the introduction of the Pye Pocket Phone personal radio, he (while on footbeat) was still required to make conference points due to the poor quality of reception on the personal radios.

I Remember When…

Memory of:
Mike Smith *(Joined Buckinghamshire in 1963, retired in 1993 from Bracknell).*

Mike remembers possibly using the first personal radio in High Wycombe for operational reasons. In 1965 he was given a Lancon personal radio which he describes as being the size of a house brick, and carried in a Sam Browne belt. He was sent along the London Road to test the range of the radio. While sending a test message from near a Police Box, an injury traffic accident occurred before his eyes.

He then used the radio to make a request for assistance and an ambulance. Unfortunately the officer at the police station was not fully conversant with the new technology, and it took a telephone call from the police box to get the full meaning of the radio message understood and acted upon.

With the full implementation of the personal radios, the police boxes became redundant and were eventually taken out of use.

COMMUNICATION

What happens now...

The radio system is one system that is used for the personal radios and the car radios.

The radio system is a digital, encrypted scheme, and in excess of 100 channels are available. This enables separate channels to be allocated to particular areas and special events.

If an incident occurs, officers attending the incident can be allocated a channel for the incident. Control of the channels is maintained by the Duty Control Room Inspector. The radio operators within Control Rooms can link channels to allow officers to hear messages from other officers.

Contact can be maintained, through the radio system, to officers at all times, and the system will log the location of the officer on the mapping system.

As the system is encrypted, people without an encrypted radio set cannot hear what is being transmitted. Providing the channel number for a force scheme is know, a officer can use the scheme to maintain contact throughout the country. The lack of radio contact as described in the journey on the M1 from Newport Pagnell to Trowell would not now occur.

Always in contact - with modern radio

Another important aspect of communication essential for the efficiency of the constable and the effectiveness of the police force, is the acquiring and the speed of communicating knowledge.

Examples of these areas, and the changes that have occurred are outlined in the memories below.

Knowledge of what has occurred or might occur

It is important that a police officer has good knowledge of what has occurred or may occur in their area.

Occurrence Books

I Remember When...

Memories of:
Geoff Allen *(Joined Reading Borough as a police cadet in 1957, appointed as a constable in 1959, retired in 1985 from Ascot)*
Jamie Eves *(Joined Berkshire as a police cadet in 1965, appointed as a constable in 1966, retired in 1997 from Taplow Traffic)*
Dick Jenkinson *(Joined Thames Valley as a police cadet in 1970, appointed as a constable in 1971, retired in 2001 from Amersham)*
John Chatterton-Ross *(Joined Thames Valley in 1987, retired in 2007 from Beaconsfield)*
Personal memory.

All remember the **Occurrence Book** and the completion of entries.

An Occurrence Book, or more often referred to as the 'OB', or occasionally 'the OB Book' (until the person realised their grammatical error!) was a means of recording on a daily basis the various incidents that had occurred or, in some cases, an entry drawing attention to what may or would be occurring on a particular date.

Geoff remembers that in Reading Borough all entries had to be completed in ink (not biro) with important aspects underlined. In Reading it was also a requirement that details of the weather were entered at certain times during the day.

KNOWLEDGE

Jamie remembers the need to cross reference entries with other pieces of information.

Dick also remembers the need for underlining important aspects.

John remembers entries as being a means for aspiring novelists to practise.

I remember that as an Inspector on a rural sub division when doing a supervisory visit to a station, I would read the station OB and initial giving the date and time of my visit. The point that John makes was often visible, however some entries were also memorable.

At one station, I read an entry relating to an indecent exposure and an indecent assault, where the offender had touched the woman's right breast. The entry continued '....It was felt by the officer reporting....' and went on to explain that if other people had not been in the vicinity, that the assault could have been more serious. However, the structure of the wording did have me wondering what actually took place with the officer reporting!

What happens now...

The Occurrence Book no longer exists.
Details of incidents that have occurred are recorded digitally in several forms, dependant upon what the incident was subsequently defined as.
All emergency calls from the public are initially received by a Control Room, either at Abingdon or Milton Keynes.
Non-emergency calls will normally be received by a Police Enquiry Centre (PEC), located at Windsor, Kidlington and Milton Keynes. The telephone number is set so that there is one emergency number (999) and one non-emergency number (101) for the whole Force area.

When an emergency call is received it is routed to the next available operator trained to deal with emergency calls - this would normally be in one of the Control Rooms. Likewise, when a non emergency call is received it is routed to the next trained operator, which would normally be in one of the PECs. All messages are recorded on the computer system and allocated a URN (Unique Reference Number). A URN message is only closed when the necessary action has been taken and recorded on the system. For certain defined incidents this may require completion of a computerised form specific to that type of defined incident.

KNOWLEDGE

Each Local Policing Area (LPA) has an Area Intelligence Team (AIT) whose daily role is to analyse details of all incidents that have occurred on the LPA. The AIT looks for trends and patterns to initiate actions with the intention of preventing further incidents and detection of offenders. In addition, each LPA has regular management meetings to review the patterns and trends and review the initial actions to see what further initiatives may be required.

Each AIT will develop a daily computerised PowerPoint briefing file that is available to teams and individuals covering that LPA. This file will include photographs of wanted people and suspect vehicles, using images retrieved from various CCTV cameras in shops or certain areas of the LPA.

The system enables one source to be used by patrol officers to gain the information of what has occurred or is likely to occur in their areas. It also enables officers based at one location, such as a Roads Policing Base, to view each of the briefing files for the areas that they may be covering when on patrol.

Crime Report Book

I Remember When...

Memory of:
Personal memory.

I remember that another book, as an information source of what had occurred on the area covered by the station, was the Crime Report Book.

When a crime occurred, a crime report was completed. The Crime Report Book had triplicate, serial numbered entries. The top copy was torn out and started the crime report file, which was held by the officer dealing, until the investigation was complete and it was approved for filing. The second entry was torn out and sent to CID administration for a central recording of the crime, and the third entry remained in the book as a source of local information. There was one crime book for each main police station, and officers had to find the current crime book and then make a manual entry.

KNOWLEDGE

What happens now…

Crime reports are one of the 'computerised forms specific to that type of defined incident' referred to in the previous entry on Occurrence Books. There is no need to 'hunt the crime book'. All crime reports are phoned through to trained officers at one of the PECs. The crime report will be the start of the crime file. Members of the public are encouraged to report crime that has occurred, using the non-emergency number (101). A trained operator will go through the form with the caller and further actions, including a visit by a police officer or Community Support Officer, will be actioned by the operator.

The computerised system can set appointment times for the visit to be made, and this is especially helpful when an officer trained to deal with a specialised type of crime is needed.

When crime is in progress, or persons are being threatened with personal injury, members of the public are advised to use the emergency number (999) so an immediate response can be made.

The Area Intelligence Team (AIT) will monitor, on a daily basis, crime that has occurred on their LPA, and crime reports are part of the analysis process described in the previous entry on Occurrence Books.

Modern Control Room

KNOWLEDGE

Knowledge of local area – Police Officers

It is important for an effective and efficient police officer to know the areas that they are patrolling.

I Remember When...

Memory of:
Dave Shillabeer *(Joined Thames Valley Police in 1971, following military service, retired in 1991 from Architectural Liaison, Pangbourne).*

Dave remembers that when first posted to Henley his Sergeant was particularly hot on constables acquiring local knowledge as soon as possible. By the end of his first month he had to know all the streets in Henley and was given a 'Met cabbie's quiz' on how to get to a street from another street. In addition, at the start of a week of night duty he was given a list of questions that had to be answered by the end of the week. Questions included the names of the pubs in the town and their landlords, times of buses and trains from Henley, and where the GWR boundary marker was at the railway station. Dave accepts it was a way of getting to know your area.

I Remember When...

Memory of:
Personal memory.

I remember, when I started as a constable at Bracknell, going out with several different constables who showed me around the area and pointed out various places and people of interest. I accept the intensity of learning was not the same as Dave Shillabear's, but it was expected for all constables to get to know their patch and the local people of note, and all officers took pride in 'their local knowledge.'

KNOWLEDGE

Checking property when on foot patrol required the development of knowledge of access to the rear of property and, in some cases, access to roof areas.

When I was a cadet at Woodley, one of the Sergeants got every constable to complete a book, giving each of the road names on the area, with the roads that led up to them or off them. This book acted as a quick reference to remember where a particular road was. However, for constables that had been at the station for some time, to have to use the book was considered a failure in their local knowledge.

When allocated a particular area or beat to patrol on a regular basis, it was important not only to know the roads on the beat but also the location of the various shops and factories, plus where various people lived and the vehicles they had access to.

What happens now...

Acquiring local knowledge is important, and the level of knowledge will depend upon the role that you perform. Community officers are responsible for a particular area so their knowledge can be very specific to that area. Officers performing response duties cover a much larger area and in some cases have to rely on the various technical aids available, such as sat navs, to assist. In addition, the control room operators have access to a digital mapping system that can also assist and give information concerning location and adjoining roads and properties.

I Remember When...

Memory of:
Dick Jenkinson *(Joined Thames Valley as a police cadet in 1970, appointed as a constable in 1971, retired in 2001 from Amersham).*

Dick remembers the beat books that were maintained at Amersham, giving the information relating to schools, business contacts and so on. This enabled officers new to a beat to acquire the knowledge that would assist them in working the beat.

KNOWLEDGE

What happens now...

Various digital files are available on computer and the internet to assist officers researching local information. Community teams have a greater knowledge of their areas than officers performing general response duties. Certainly, through computer technology, the availability of local information is greater than it used to be, and it is then dependant upon individual officers as to how much general detail they wish to remember.

Knowledge of people

I Remember When...

Memories of:
Geoff Allen *(Joined Reading Borough as a police cadet in 1957, appointed as a constable in 1959 retired in 1985 from Ascot)*
Dave Marchant *(Joined Thames Valley in 1973, retired in 2003 from Reading.)*
Personal memory.

We all remember that an important element of police work is knowing people. If you were patrolling a beat and a person was behaving other than what might be expected, this led to the 'policeman's instinct' and often led to the detection or prevention of a crime.

It would be normal to speak to such people and find out who they were and what they might be doing. Details would be recorded, especially when people were seen at night.

With the introduction of the radio system - both in the car and later the personal radio - it was possible to check the details of the person with the police station or the control room.

Most divisional stations would have a 'Collator' who later became the 'Local Intelligence Officer' *(LIO)*. Here, all details of local people who had committed crime or were suspected of a crime were logged. On a Force wide basis, a similar central role was performed by the Force Criminal Record Office *(CRO)* or the national CRO at Scotland Yard. The level at which you requested checks on the person would be dependant upon the level of suspicion raised as you spoke to them.

However, the requested checks were checks on manual records and would take several minutes and were not always available 24 hours a day or seven days a week. Communication skills were developed both in establishing the facts of who a person was, where they lived and what they were doing, and also keeping the person talking and staying with you while the checks with the LIO or CRO were being made through the radio operator.

What happens now...

The need to know people, who they are and what they are doing obviously still exists, and good communication skills are essential. What is different is the speed and the levels of checks that can be made It still originates with a radio request to the Control Room, but the control room operator now has all the information available through the various computer databases they can directly access. The overall speed and detail of access has greatly increased.

What has changed is the legislation that enables the process of 'stop and search' and also the requirements to record such searches and the reasons for them. The 'policeman's instinct' is still there, but the accountability and the recording for using it has increased.

Knowledge of local area – Radio Operators

It is important for an effective control room operator to have knowledge of the areas that they are controlling and the units available for them to deploy. How the acquiring of this knowledge has changed is outlined in the memories below.

I Remember When...

Memory of:
Blackney Chambers *(Joined Buckinghamshire in 1949, retired in 1979 from Slough)*
Personal memory.

KNOWLEDGE

Blackney remembers that with the introduction of radios into police cars a control room was set up in the Buckinghamshire Headquarters at Aylesbury. In order to plot locations of incidents and vehicles and effectively direct and control vehicles, a large map (the size of a billiard table) was set under glass in the control room.

I remember that as personal radios were introduced each main police station had control of their local personal radio scheme. The main stations developed their own control rooms, staffed by constables, and in some cases assisted by civilian operators.

I remember that as a Shift Inspector in Reading, the team in the Reading Control Room were part of my shift and supervision responsibilities. Officers were only deployed to Control Room duties if they had good local knowledge of the area and good communication skills. The only items to assist them when deploying units to an incident and controlling the incident were paper maps and other manual record cards, but the most effective element was their local knowledge.

What happens now…

The radio system operators are based in a Control Room either at Abingdon or Milton Keynes, and can either be a police officer or a civilian control room operator. They may not have an in-depth knowledge of an area, but they have immediate access to the digital mapping system and other digital files. The mapping system can be viewed at various levels, the greater of which will give details of property names or numbers, and show footpaths as well as minor tracks and roads. The location of an incident, with the Unique Reference Number (URN) relating to the incident, will be shown on the map, as will the location of police units in the area, which is displayed and updated using the Global Positioning System (GPS).

The technical skills of the operator in using the technology available to them can overcome lack of local knowledge.

KNOWLEDGE

Time and location calls

I Remember When...

Memory of:
Personal memory.

During 1970/71 while I was on the North East Traffic Area *(NETA)* at Bletchley. Kidlington Control Room introduced 'Time and Location Calls'. This was a method of keeping their records updated as to which vehicles were still 'booked on' and where they were.

The controller would first call each of the divisional vehicles they had booked on, in divisional and numerical order, and then call the traffic vehicles, again in the divisional order in which they were working. Covering 'J' divisional area, we were one of the last vehicles to be called. The whole process could take between ten and 15 minutes to complete.

I can remember that, if on general patrol, and not committed with an incident, that I would prepare for my response at the start of the Time and Location call process. I would find an interesting sounding village name, in the area I was patrolling, possibly one that the operator may not have heard of. My favourite, if I was in the north of the Division around Newport Pagnell or Olney was the village of Newton Blossomville. I would then make my way there. When called I could, truthfully reply "Tango 2, Newton Blossomville". Often the response was "Tango 2 repeat location..?".

This process ensured three things: I developed my knowledge of my patrol area; the village of Newton Blossomville would occasionally see a traffic patrol car; and if the Control Room Operator looked the location up on their map, they would get to know the area they were controlling.

KNOWLEDGE

What happens now...

With the mapping system mentioned in the above entry, the radio operator is visually shown the location of all units who have booked on with the control room. A time and location call is no longer required.

Weather reports

I Remember When...

Memory of:
Andy Sharples *(Joined Thames Valley in 1969, retired in 2000 from Bletchley).*

Andy remembers the occasions when, especially in the early hours of a cold winter's morning, Control Room would request weather reports from patrolling vehicles.

In the early hours of one morning, while in a lay by on the A413 near Buckingham, Andy and his colleague received a request for a weather report. They reported that it was foggy with visibility limited to 50 yards.

Having completed checks with other vehicles, the radio operator informed him that they were the only vehicle reporting fog. It was then that they realised it was condensation on the vehicle's windscreen!

What happens now...

Today there is a great deal of technical monitoring and reporting of weather conditions, which will be available to Control Room operators, but it is still important to report isolated weather problems such as ice or fog, that can occur in various 'hollows'.

KNOWLEDGE

Knowledge and information on motor vehicles

Knowledge about a motor vehicle, for example:

* *Who is the registered owner?*

* *Has the vehicle been reported stolen?*

* *Has the vehicle been involved in crime?*

* *Is the vehicle insured?*

Is essential for efficient policing. For memories covering knowledge and motor vehicles please see the entry POLICE DUTIES – and motor vehicles.

PAY AND ALLOWANCES

Several allowances are paid to police officers in addition to their basic salary. Listed below are some of the memories concerning allowances that were paid.

Paste Allowance

I Remember When...

Memory of:
Cyril Wise *(joined Buckinghamshire in 1947, retired in 1975 from Aylesbury Traffic).*

Cyril remembers that while at Bletchley in 1952, while performing administration duties, he was responsible for maintaining a large manual pay sheet detailing all officers on the Division. It recorded their salary and any special allowance that were applicable or claimed by each officer. Uniform officers, although provided with a uniform, were paid a boot and shoe allowance as they were responsible for the provision of their footwear. CID officers who were required to wear plain clothes were paid a plain clothes allowance. Officers who needed a pedal cycle to complete their cycle patrol duties, which they provided themselves, were paid a cycle allowance.

One allowance that Cyril particularly remembers was one that was paid to all constables who were resident in rural beat houses. This was a '**Paste Allowance**' of one shilling (5p) per quarter (every three months) for paste in order that they could stick up the required posters and notices to the notice boards outside their police houses.

All officers were paid fortnightly and their wages were paid in cash, in pay packets.

PAY AND ALLOWANCES

Boot Allowance

I Remember When...

Memory of:
Ken Amery *(joined Berkshire as a police cadet in 1964, appointed as a constable in 1966, retired in 1996 from Windsor).*

Ken remembers that although all officers were provided with a uniform, they had to supply their own footwear, which was normally black boots. For this, a **'boot allowance'** was paid.

Cycle Allowance

I Remember When...

Memories of:
Ken Amery *(joined Berkshire as a police cadet in 1964, appointed as a constable in 1966, retired in 1996 from Windsor)*
Cameron Floate *(Joined Oxfordshire in 1951, transferred to Berkshire in 1956, retired in 1981 from Maidenhead).*

Ken remembers that where an officer had to provide their own bicycle in order to carry out their duties, a 'cycle allowance' was paid.

Cameron remembers claiming the cycle allowance when he was posted to the rural beat at Wargrave and had to provide his own pedal cycle to patrol the area.

What happens now...

Various allowances still occur, which are added to the basic salary of police officers. These allowances are under review, so I have not gone into any detail, however paste and cycle allowances are no longer paid.

PAY AND ALLOWANCES

Coroner's Allowance

I Remember When...

I Remember When...

Memories of:
Cyril Wise *(joined Buckinghamshire in 1947, retired in 1975 from Aylesbury Traffic)*
Ken Amery *(joined Berkshire as a police cadet in 1964, appointed as a constable in 1966, retired in 1996 from Windsor)*
Personal memory.

Cyril remembers an allowance that could be claimed from the Coroner when you dealt with a sudden death and had to accompany the body to the mortuary and prepare the body for identification by a relative. For a normal sudden death the allowance was ten shillings (50p), but for a badly injured or decomposed body one pound (£1) could be claimed.

    Ken and I can remember this being available in Berkshire. It should be mentioned that at this time there were no separate officers working as Coroner's Officers. If you were sent to a sudden death you were required to see the whole process through. In most cases, mortuaries were not part of a hospital, but often single-brick buildings maintained by the local council. *(Also see entry under Police Duties – Sudden Death).*

What happens now...

Although police officers still attend sudden deaths, when the body is removed from the scene it will go to a mortuary, where civilian Coroners Officers will normally deal with the identification process. No allowance is paid for dealing with a sudden death.

PAY AND ALLOWANCES

Excise Allowance

I Remember When...

Memory of:
Cyril Wise *(joined Buckinghamshire in 1947, retired in 1975 from Aylesbury Traffic).*

Cyril remembers paying out and, in some cases claiming allowances relating to the detection of certain offences. He remembers that for no dog licence, two shillings and six pence (12 ½ p) was paid, and for no firearms certificate five shillings (25p) was paid. He remembers being disappointed, when, on one occasion, he discovered a person with several unlicensed weapons. He was hoping for five shillings for each firearm, but was informed it was only one payment of five shillings for the detection.

What happens now...

A dog licence is no longer required, and no allowance is paid relating to detection of offences.

Additional Rest Days (ARD) and Extra Rest Days (ERD)

I Remember When...

Memory of:
Personal memory.

I remember when I first joined Berkshire Constabulary as a constable in 1966 that during the winter period you were required to work two of your eight rest days per month. These were referred to as Additional Rest Days *(ARDs)* and in the summer months a further requirement was made to work an extra rest day, which was referred to as an Extra Rest Day *(ERD)*. This was to ensure that there was sufficient manpower available to cover the shift rotas.

Payment received for working these rest days was welcomed due to the relatively low salary that we received. When I joined in 1966, at the age of 19, my salary was £700 per year.

If you worked over your normal duty hours in a day you did not receive paid overtime, but could claim for time off in lieu. Overtime was only paid when the additional hours worked related to a major incident, such as a murder investigation or a special event, e.g. Royal Ascot Races or Henley Regatta. These had to be declared a 'Special Event' in order for the overtime to be paid.

What happens now...

Overtime allowance is paid to constables and sergeants, but the need to work the overtime has to be approved.

Paid weekly, in cash

I Remember When...

Memories of:
George Brown *(Joined Berkshire in 1954, retired in 1984 from Headquarters Operations)*
Dick Allen *(Joined Berkshire as a boy clerk in 1948 at Newbury - later role changed to police cadet - following return from national service, appointed as a constable in 1952, retired in 1984 from Banbury).*

George remembers that, when he joined, wages in Berkshire were paid weekly in cash. The Superintendent often delivered the pay packets to the police stations and rural beat houses, while making a weekly supervisory visit.

PAY AND ALLOWANCES

George, remembers that his Superintendent was a keen gardener and would give him, the occupant of a rural beat house, free advice when he inspected his garden. The advice was expected to be taken.

Dick remembers that as the Admin Constable at Abingdon and later the Admin Sergeant in the Berkshire Headquarters, one of his responsibilities was preparing the weekly pay packets. This involved calculating what each person would be paid that week, and working out the denomination of the notes and coins that would be required to make up that pay packet. He then had to calculate how many of each denomination he would require to complete all the pay packets, and order this from the bank.

He then had to collect the cash from the bank, prepare the individual wage slips and make up each pay packet. They had to be ready for the weekly Pay Day, either for individual collection or for delivery to the various stations or offices where the persons awaiting their pay packets would be.

Dick remembers that, when he was at the Berkshire Constabulary Headquarters at Sulhamstead, the weekly pay run to collect monies from the bank in Theale consisted of him and a civillian clerk in one car, followed by a police dog handler in a police vehicle. This ensured the security of the police wages, although he was surprised when he saw that the money was delivered to the Theale bank by a bank employee bringing the cash by bus from the Reading branch to the bank in Theale.

What happens now...

All pay is paid monthly direct to bank or building society accounts. Each month, an 'All users' email message is sent out confirming that the money has been paid in and that salary slips are available to view online. Each employee has an individual email account and can access their salary information online using their personal access code.

Police Cadets

Police cadets were present in of all the constituent Forces when they amalgamated into the Thames Valley Constabulary in 1968, and remained until the regular cadet force was disbanded in 1984.

The forerunner of the police cadet was the Junior Clerk, later referred to as a Boy Clerk. Police cadets started in Berkshire Constabulary in 1948.

The idea of a police cadet system was to enable young people to join the police service between the ages of 16 and 18. Constables could only be appointed at the age of 19. Cadets were effectively civillian employees and most of their work was linked to administration roles. Time spent as a police cadet provided an insight into the role of the police and police work.

Memories of former cadets, and the types of duties they performed, are outlined on the following pages.

POLICE CADETS

Junior Clerks

I Remember When…

Memory of:
Maurice Hedges *(joined Berkshire as a junior clerk in 1940, appointed following national service as a constable in 1946, retired in 1975 from Wokingham).*

Maurice remembers that as a Junior Clerk in the Berkshire Headquarters at Reading in 1940 he worked in the Telephone Room which was under the supervision of a police constable.

Boy Clerks

I Remember When…

Memory of:
Dick Allen *(Joined Berkshire as a boy clerk in 1948 at Newbury - later role changed to police cadet - following return from national service appointed as a constable in 1952, retired in 1984 from Banbury).*

Dick remembers starting as a Boy Clerk at Newbury and cycling to and from his home in East Ilsley on a daily basis, a distance of nine miles each way. This enforced exercise was sometimes relieved with a lift home by the police mobile crew, driving a Sunbeam Talbot Tourer motor car. His bicycle was strapped to the boot of the car. He later obtained a lift from the AWRE Harwell drivers (rewarded with a packet of cigarettes) who regularly went between Harwell and Newbury.

Shortly after starting as a Boy Clerk, the position was changed to the newly-created Police Cadet. At the time, cadets were allocated numbers and **Dick** was Cadet 10 in the Berkshire Constabulary.

Police Cadets

I Remember When…

Memory of:
John Harker *(Joined Oxfordshire as a police cadet in 1958, appointed as a constable in 1961, retired in 1987 from District Police Training Centre, Cwmbran).*

John also remembers that cycling was the only method of transport from his home in Stadhampton to his station at Watlington - a distance of six-and-a-half miles, which he did on a daily basis.

I Remember When…

Memory of:
Personal memory.

I remember that when I first started, as a police cadet in 1963 in the Berkshire Control Room at Sulhamstead, a coach was provided for staff who were working 0900-1700 shifts to travel from Reading to Sulhamstead. This was because the Berkshire Headquarters moved from Reading to Sulhamstead in 1952 and civilian staff working in Reading were assisted in transport to Sulhamstead.

When I started working 0800-1600 and 1400-2200 shifts in the Control Room I used my motor scooter, however when this broke down I had to cycle 10 miles each way.

POLICE CADETS

Police Cadet duties

Black out duties (Junior Clerk)

I Remember When...

Memory of:
Maurice Hedges *(joined Berkshire as a junior clerk in 1940, appointed following national service, as a constable in 1946, retired in 1975 from Wokingham).*

Maurice remembers that, as a junior clerk in 1940, one of his duties when working a 2pm-10pm shift was to ensure that the 'black out blinds' for the building were in place. On one of the first occasions he was required to do this he had problems in the ladies toilet, which was in the main block of the Berkshire Headquarters. The windows were high up, above the sink, and he had difficulty reaching the blind. Using his developing initiative, he stood on the sink to reach the blind. The sink came away from the wall, and he could not replace it back to its original state. Under the supervision of the duty constable, he typed a report concerning the incident and was summoned before the Deputy Chief Constable where he received strong advice about his future conduct. The experience assisted his developing initiative!

Morse code and fire fighting training (Junior Clerk)

I Remember When...

Memory of:
Maurice Hedges *(joined Berkshire as a junior clerk in 1940, appointed following national service, as a constable in 1946, retired in 1975 from Wokingham).*

Maurice remembers that as a junior clerk in 1940 in the Berkshire Headquarters, he was trained in Morse code (should its use be necessary due to the war).

POLICE CADETS

Maurice also remembers in 1941 that due to the possibility of incendiary bombs being dropped, all police officers and civilians were trained in putting incendiaries out by using a stirrup pump.

Pieces of an incendiary device were set alight in the centre of a yard and a person had to crawl along the ground with the end of the stirrup pump in one hand and aim the jet of water onto the incendiary.

He states no person was exempt from the training, which was even completed by the Chief Constable.

Berkshire Constabulary helmet plate

POLICE CADETS

Cadet duties at Watlington

I Remember When...

Memory of:
John Harker *(Joined Oxfordshire as a police cadet in 1958, appointed as a constable in 1961, retired in 1987 from Police District Training Centre, Cwmbran).*

John remembers that his duties as a cadet at Watlington were initially answering the telephone, taking messages and making the tea. The Inspector would often send him on errands to the shops, which occasionally also required him to take the Inspector's four-year-old daughter.

John managed to go out on occasions with police constables in the station van. He particularly remembers one afternoon going out with the Sergeant to a house in a rural village to a report of an old man jumping into his well. As John explains 'The well was no more than a large pipe, about two feet wide. Looking down the well you could see the top of the head of the missing man. That was enough for me! I went back and sat in the van. I could hear the Sergeant talking to the ambulance crew that had just arrived, "How are we going to get him out? Someone will have to go down on a rope. Where's that boy?"

John confirms that he was lowered down on a rope, but on reaching the body managed to convince the people lowering him that he could not do what was being asked, so he was hauled back to the surface. The body was later retrieved by other means.

Cadet duties at Newbury and Wokingham

I Remember When...

Memory of:
Dick Allen *(Joined Berkshire as a boy clerk in 1948 at Newbury - later role changed to police cadet - following return from national service appointed as a constable in 1952, retired in 1984 from Banbury).*

Dick remembers starting as a Boy Clerk at Newbury in February 1948. The job title was then changed to Police Cadet. He worked 0600-1400 and 1400-2200 shifts.

POLICE CADETS

When the job title changed, from Boy Clerk to Police Cadet, there was little change in the duties. He was required to take and record messages, answer the telephone, work the switchboard, answer public enquiries received at the counter and carry out general admin duties, which included typing reports, memos and any other documents.

Where copies of messages or reports were required carbon paper had to be used. Carbon paper was kept in a box. He remembers that on one occasion he was called to the Superintendent's office.

A comment had been made that he had failed to treat the carbon paper correctly, often returning carbon paper to the box without ensuring the paper was not creased in the process. It was pointed out to Dick, by the Superintendent, that a sheet of creased carbon paper could not be used and that he was wasting money. It was obviously an important matter that the Superintendent felt he had to personally deal with!

Dick later transferred to Wokingham Police Station where his hours of duty were 0700-1500 and 1500-2200. The reduction of hours on the late turn shift were made up by having to work on Saturdays.

Duties were very similar to those at Newbury. Like Newbury, Wokingham was a Divisional station with section stations at Sonning (later Woodley), Twyford, Bracknell and Crowthorne. The first task each morning was to obtain a list of officers on duty at each station and the conference points they had been allocated. Dick then had to type these up so that they were available in the office at Wokingham.

If a call was received requiring a constable to attend, the sheet would be checked to find the next available constable on the section who could attend the call. If no constable was available on the section, if necessary, the availability of officers on adjoining sections was checked, they would be contacted and would have to cycle into the adjoining section.

Although each Divisional Station had the availability of a car and a driver, if the car and driver were out they were not contactable as radios in cars were not introduced until 1952, and personal radios were only introduced between 1965 and 1967 *(See entry under COMMUNICATION – Conference Points)*.

During his last three months at Wokingham, prior to leaving to undertake National Service, Dick performed duty as a police cadet in the CID office. In recognition of his role in CID he was allowed to wear plain clothes. His duties entailed general admin and typing, and the typing enabled him to gain knowledge of the content and composition of crime and court files. This greatly assisted when he returned from National Service and was appointed a constable.

POLICE CADETS

Cadet duties in the Berkshire Headquarters Control Room

I Remember When...

Memory of:
Personal memory.

I remember that when I started in 1963 as a police cadet in the Berkshire Control Room, I was part of a team of three, (four if we were lucky) The team consisted of a Sergeant, who was the duty officer, and then either a constable, a civilian clerk or a police cadet making up the rest of the team. There was a Monday to Friday daytime switch board operator - Barbara Hunt.

When Barbara was off or having a meal break it was the police cadet who was first reserve to do the switchboard duty. Barbara made the morning and afternoon tea, and this role was part of my duty when Barbara was off. *(See entry under COMMUNICATIONS - Telephones)*

As a member of the team, I would operate as controller on the Force radio scheme, man the teleprinter room, or do administration duties such as maintaining the stolen car index *(See entry under POLICE DUTIES – and motor vehicles)* or recording the notification of movements of abnormal loads through Berkshire.

The role was a very operational role, and when Royal Ascot Races or Royal Henley Regatta took place I was the junior member of the control room team that worked the local police control at the event.

I remember that at Henley Regatta, one of the duties I was given was to find CID officers if they were required. I was introduced to the three Detectives at the beginning of the event. This was prior to the introduction of personal radios and, although they were required to check in at regular intervals, my task was finding them if urgently required between the check-in times. Good practice in identification.

In my last year's duties at Henley Regatta (1965) the local police control, which operated from a purpose-built caravan, was issued with a 'walkie talkie' set. This consisted of two identical radios - one which acted as a base station control in the caravan, the other which could be issued to a person who could go out but maintain contact with the control – the forerunner of the personal radio scheme.

The sets were large and strapped to the carrier's back. An aerial about three feet long extended upwards from the set. On occasions, especially when out walking towards the fair, which was situated outside of the Regatta enclosures, I often heard someone whistling the tune of 'Z Cars' as I passed!

Cadet duties at Woodley

I Remember When…

Memory of:
Personal memory.

In late 1965, **I** transferred as a police cadet from the Control Room at Berkshire Headquarters to the section station at Woodley. As I was over 18, I was permitted to go out on patrol with police officers although the main part of my duties consisted of answering the telephone and assisting the duty constable in manning the public enquiry office. Washing police vehicles, cleaning out the stray dog kennels, feeding stray dogs, and getting meals for prisoners from Stewarts Transport Café, were also part of the role.

On one occasion I was out with a constable doing unoccupied property checks *(See entry under POLICE DUTIES – Notification of unoccupied property).* On this occasion it was just getting dark and we were checking property in rural Earley, (now the Lower Earley Housing Estate). We had driven down a lane to an isolated detached bungalow. The constable told me to check the property while he turned the police van around. I approached the bungalow, which stood in a large, somewhat overgrown garden. It had a porch, and I tried the door handle expecting to find the porch locked. It was not. In the gloom, I opened the door to check the inner main door…and froze! Once my heart rate returned to normal, I realised that I was looking at a *six foot plus, grizzly bear that was stood up with its arms around a tree trunk*. It looked very realistic, especially in the dim light.

I confirmed the security of the front door and the rest of the property, and returned to the police van. The constable could see my approach and greeted me with 'You saw it then?' I will not enter details of my reply.

POLICE CADETS

Cadet duties in Reading

I Remember When…

Memory of:
Geoff Allen *(Joined Reading Borough as a police cadet in 1957, appointed as a constable in 1959, retired from Ascot in 1985)*
Personal memory.

Geoff remembers, on Saturdays, as a police cadet, performing pedestrian control duties in Broad Street, Reading. **I** remember as a teenager visiting the town centre on a Saturday, seeing the police cadets performing the duty. Broad Street was the main road through the town and the main centre for shopping. In addition, it was the main bus pick up point and interchange of bus routes. Traffic light controlled pedestrian crossings had not been invented so, in order to keep traffic moving, the two pedestrian crossings were under police control during peak times. Each crossing had one police constable assisted by one or two police cadets.

Reading Borough helmet plate

POLICE CADETS

Cadet duties at Royal Ascot Races and Henley Regatta

I Remember When...

Memories of:
Ken Amery *(Joined Berkshire as a police cadet in 1964, appointed as a constable in 1966, retired in 1996 from Windsor)*
Personal memory.

Ken can remember that in 1965, as a police cadet in Berkshire, at Royal Ascot Races, cadets assisted in the provision of catering for police officers performing duty at the event. He remembers his main role was making cheese rolls and clearing the tables.

Ken remembers that there was a snack bar for police officers and another for other people working at the races. There was also a drinks bar. Cooked food was also supplied in the snack bars, the food being prepared by police constables brought in for this duty.

Other police cadets were involved in assisting in the preparation of the food and clearing tables in the snack and drinks bar. Ken describes the work as hard, long, but enjoyable.

Ken did similar duties at Royal Ascot in 1966. On this occasion, the cadets stayed in the dormitory on the first floor of the old Ascot Police Station. The building had originally been built to accommodate police officers attending Royal Ascot Races. Ken particularly remembers this year as, now being 18, he went into the bar with the other cadets at the end of the day's work and can remember the cadets being bought a drink by the Chief Constable.

I remember some of my fellow cadets performing the catering duties both at Royal Ascot and at Henley Regatta. I count myself lucky to have been a cadet in the Berkshire Control Room that was set up at these events - although part of the duty was getting the tea and cheese rolls for staff in the control room!

Police duties

The following sections deal with memories about police duties, from the hours of duty through to the various duties performed during those hours.

Police duties - Hours of duty – Paid and unpaid

It is often said that a policeman is on duty 24 hours a day, however there are the paid and unpaid elements of that 24 hours. Examples of some of the duties and some of the unpaid elements are provided in the following memories, with some comparisons with the situation today.

Split Shifts

I Remember When...

Memories of:
George Brown *(Joined Berkshire in 1954, retired in 1984 from Headquarters Operations)*
Arthur Chaplin *(Joined Berkshire in 1949, retired in 1984 from Newbury)*
Cyril Wise *(Joined Buckinghamshire in 1947, retired in 1965 from Aylesbury, Traffic).*

George and **Arthur** can both remember working split shifts as rural beat constables. Shifts included a 1400-1800 followed by 2200-0200, another being 1000-1300 followed by 1800-2300. George points out that even when off duty, as a rural beat constable, you were expected to answer the telephone and enquiries made direct to the house. While you were away from your house on patrol, this was a role carried out by the rural constable's wife.

    Cyril, when stationed at Bletchley, remembers rural beat constables performing similar split shifts to those that George and Arthur were performing in Berkshire.

POLICE DUTIES

What happens now…

Split shifts have not been rostered as part of a duty rota for many years. All shifts are a continuous tour of duty which includes time for a meal break.

Extended shifts

I Remember When…

Memory of:
Ron Angell *(Joined Berkshire in 1958, retired in 1988 from Bracknell).*

Ron remembers working as an aide to CID at Maidenhead in 1962. On a particular day he reported for duty at 0900 and went to Reading Quarter Sessions, returning at 1730, which was eight-and-a-half hours - a full day's duty. However, he was told to report back for observation duties at 2200 and then worked through to 0600. He worked a total of 16 ½ hours but without any compensation for the additional hours.

Duty rota in Woodley CID

I Remember When…

Memory of:
Personal memory.

I remember that in 1969 I was appointed a Temporary Detective Constable at Woodley. The CID duty rota consisted of M & A, M & E, and M, A, & E, and occasionally A & E.

POLICE DUTIES

'M' was Mornings that started at 0800, 'A' was Afternoon that started at 1400 and 'E' was Evenings that started at 1800. This was the time you were expected to be there. There did not appear to be a finishing time, you went when you had completed at least eight hours. The rota for the week often exceeded the 40-hour week, but it was necessary to provide sufficient cover. You were not expected to claim for the additional hours worked, unless it was connected with a major inquiry.

What happens now...

There are regulations covering what additional hours worked can be claimed as paid overtime, and working of overtime must be approved. Overtime worked can be claimed for payment or time off in lieu. Officers are not expected to work hours for which no compensation would be given.

Quick change overs

I Remember When...

Memory of:
Personal memory.

I, like many uniform officers, remember the three shift system, nights (2200-0600), lates (1400-2200) and earlys (0600-1400) which provided cover over the 24-hour period. Normally, a four-week duty rota would involve one quick changeover, which is when you had only eight hours between one shift and the next. This normally occurred at the end of a tour of nights when you finished at 0600, but returned for a 1400-2200 shift. This enabled you to have a full rest day, rather than if the rest day was immediately after the night shift when some of the day would be spent sleeping.

When I went to Reading in 1976, the shift rota involved three quick changeovers in the four week period. One was after nights, the other two were used to split up having to work seven consecutive late or early turn shifts.

POLICE DUTIES

This was done by one week, after three 1400-2200 shifts, finishing one at 2200 and returning the next day at 0600 and working four 0600-1400 shifts. The next part of the rota the same quick change over took place after working four 1400-2200 shifts, with the quick changeover to 0600-1400 shift followed by three further 0600-1400 shifts, before a much needed three rest days over a weekend to finish the four week rota.

What happens now...

The uniform duty rota has a variance of shifts, some of which are slightly more than eight hours. Some of the shifts provide an overlap with another shift to increase cover at known operational peak periods e.g. Friday and Saturday nights. The main duty system is no longer based on individual station rotas, but effectively a Force wide system. It is currently under review in order to improve cover at anticipated peak operational periods. There are different shift rotas for specialist teams such as Roads Policing and Community Teams.

Hours of duty – Major Event – Royal Ascot Races

I Remember When...

Memory of:
Dick Allen *(Joined Berkshire as a boy clerk in 1948, at Newbury - later role changed to police cadet - following return from national service appointed as a constable in 1952, retired in 1984 from Banbury).*

Dick remembers that when he was stationed at Ascot, while the Royal Ascot Races were on, the officers based at Ascot worked a 0600-1000 followed by a 1800-2200 or 2200-0700 shift. Policing of Ascot between 1000 and 1800 was covered by the policing detail connected with Ascot Races.

POLICE DUTIES

Dick also remembers the hours that had to be worked by officers who were nominated for Royal Ascot duties. They normally had to be at Ascot for 1000 and did not finish the actual duty at Ascot until the crowds had left, which could be 1900 or later. Either side of these hours they had to travel to and from Ascot, which was normally in coaches. For officers from the West of the county at Faringdon, Shrivenham and Wantage (which were in Berkshire up until 1972), this required an early start and late finish with an early start the next day. As Royal Ascot was declared a major event, it was one of the few occasions that the additional hours worked were paid.

Parading for duty

I Remember When...

Memories of:
Ken Amery *(Joined Berkshire as a police cadet in 1964, appointed as a constable in 1966, retired in 1996 from Windsor)*
Geoff Allen *(Joined Reading Borough as a police cadet in 1957, appointed as a constable in 1959, retired in 1985 from Ascot)*
Cameron Floate *(Joined Oxfordshire in 1951, retired in 1981 from Maidenhead)*
Rodney Watson *(Joined Berkshire as a police cadet in 1964, appointed as a constable in 1965, retired in 1995 from Taplow Traffic)*
Personal memory.

All can remember the requirement to parade 15 minutes prior to the start of a shift. The nature of the parade varied depending upon the station - some being very formal, based on military lines.

This 15 minutes was unpaid, and where you were responsible for taking the parade, the time preparing for the parade had to be added on, again unpaid. For example as an Shift Inspector in Reading for a 2200-0600 shift, I arrived at 2130 to liaise with the Inspector going off duty and made sure that the Sergeants had all the necessary information for the 2145 parade.

POLICE DUTIES

What happens now...

All duties are set up and managed through a computer programme called a Duty Management System (DMS). This displays an individual officer's tour of duty on a given date, in accordance with the overall duty rota. It then monitors the hours that the officer actually works as the officers are booked on and booked off the system by their manager. A code is given when an officer is engaged in a special duty.

A shift starts at the nominated time for the shift. A team of officers assembles at the nominated time for the start of shift in a briefing room to be briefed by the team sergeant. This briefing takes place at the start of the shift, not 15 minutes prior to the start, however officers will have arrived earlier and will be ready to be deployed direct from the briefing.

At the conclusion of the shift, where the officer does not finish at the nominated end shift time, there are regulations concerning what counts as overtime, for time off or payment, but this additional working time must be authorised, which is shown on the DMS system by an overtime code being entered by the shift manager.

Basically the first 30 minutes do not count for overtime unless a certain level of this uncoded overtime is worked in a given period.

Reading Borough - annual parade Forbury Gardens (late 1950s/early 60s)

68

POLICE DUTIES

Preparing Sulhamstead House as the Berkshire Headquarters

I Remember When...

Memory of:
Dick Allen *(Joined Berkshire as a boy clerk in 1948, at Newbury - later role changed to police cadet - following return from national service appointed as a constable in 1952, retired in 1984 from Banbury).*

Dick remembers that when the Berkshire Constabulary was preparing Sulhamstead House and grounds ready for the move of the Berkshire Constabulary Headquarters, and staff from Reading. Staff were encouraged to give time on their days off to go to Sulhamstead and assist in preparing the house and grounds. This preparation work was unpaid, but officers were informed that their contribution *(or non-contribution)* would be recognised.

Evening work in Berkshire Headquarters

I Remember When...

Memory of:
Dick Allen *(Joined Berkshire as a boy clerk in 1948, at Newbury - later role changed to police cadet - following return from national service appointed as a constable in 1952, retired in 1984 from Banbury).*

Dick remembers that when stationed at Sulhamstead as the Administration Sergeant that, like some other officers stationed there, his workload could take more than an eight hour day. His Superintendent often returned to his office in the evening and expected his police staff to do the same. No overtime was paid for the additional hours.

POLICE DUTIES

Living in a Rural Beat House

I Remember When...

Memories of:
Arthur Chaplin *(Joined Berkshire in 1949, retired in 1984 from Newbury)*
Cameron Floate *(Joined Oxfordshire in 1951, transferred to Berkshire in 1956, retired in 1981 from Maidenhead)*
George Brown *(Joined Berkshire in 1954, retired in 1984 from HQ Operations).*

All remember living in rural police houses. In addition to performing split shifts effectively they were never off duty as they were required to answer telephone calls and visitors to the house. When they were away from the house working, this role fell to their wife.

Telephone cover

I Remember When...

Memory of:
Dick Allen *(Joined Berkshire as a boy clerk in 1948, at Newbury - later role changed to police cadet - following return from national service appointed as a constable in 1952, retired in 1984 from Banbury)*
Personal memory.

Both Dick and I can remember the additional roles that came with living in police houses attached to small section stations. All the additional hours worked were unpaid.

    Dick, in the late 1950s, was posted to a house adjoining the section station at Bracknell (before the development of Bracknell). The police officers on the section performed duties between 0800 and 0200, with the police station manned from 0800-2400. After 2400, the telephone was transferred to the occupants of one of two police houses that adjoined the station. The resident constable with responsibility for covering the calls on a particular night would be shown on the duty sheet. When you were nominated to receive calls you were required to be at home.

POLICE DUTIES

Between 2400 and 0200 if a call required the attendance of a police officer, you could contact the divisional station at Wokingham who would contact an officer on their point. After 0200 if an officer was required to attend, you had to get up and attend yourself.

I can remember a similar situation when I was at Twyford in 1966 and 1967. Here, the telephone duty was covered by four officers. The police office was not manned every evening and the telephone was transferred to the police houses when the station was unmanned. On the evenings that you were shown on the duty sheet as telephone cover it meant that you had to remain in your house and could not go out.

With the introduction of radios in police vehicles, it was easier to contact officers on patrol. After 0200 the section was covered by Woodley.

No additional pay was received for this duty, even when there was a requirement to attend yourself.

What happens now...

Over recent years, with the removal of the provision of police accommodation as part of officers conditions of service, there are no longer officers living in rural beat houses, or houses on small section stations.
The telephone system now has only two main numbers for the whole of the Thames Valley Police area - the emergency number (999), and non- emergency number (101). These calls are answered either in a Control Room at Abingdon or Milton Keynes or in a Police Enquiry Centre (PEC) at Windsor, Kidlington or Milton Keynes.
In addition, there is the direct dial system which enables calls to be made to a specific extension number.

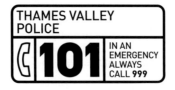

THAMES VALLEY POLICE

101 IN AN EMERGENCY ALWAYS CALL 999

POLICE DUTIES

Police duties – and motor vehicles

Since the motor car was invented there have been laws to govern its use. Use of motor vehicles in crime increased as vehicles became more readily available.

Police work has therefore been closely linked to the motor vehicle, both in enforcement of the law relating to motor vehicles, and the criminal use of motor vehicles. Outlined below are some of the memories linked to the performance of this role.

Obtaining information if a car had been stolen

Information on whether a motor vehicle has been stolen, or suspected of being involved in crime is very important for effective policing. The memories outlined below illustrate how this was obtained.

I Remember When…

Memory of:
Personal memory.

I remember that as a member of staff in the Berkshire Constabulary Control Room, one important duty was maintaining the stolen vehicle Rotadex file. A card (blue) was completed for each reported stolen car and a similar card (red) for each vehicle involved in crime. These were clipped into the circular drum type files, and filed under the initial letter of the index number and then numerically. Information for completing the cards came from two sources i) teleprinter messages received from stations within Berkshire or surrounding forces or ii) from Supplement F of Police Gazette.

Police Gazette was produced daily and originated from Scotland Yard, who had responsibility for collating criminal information on a national basis.

Supplement F contained details of vehicles stolen, and date and place from where stolen. It also contained details of stolen vehicles that had been recovered and had to be removed from the stolen vehicle file. It would take an average of ten days for a stolen vehicle to appear in Supplement F and be entered into the stolen vehicle file.

POLICE DUTIES

Patrolling police vehicles, equipped with radio, would ask the radio controller for a stolen vehicle check, and a check would be made in the Rotadex stolen vehicle file. Telephone calls were also received from stations throughout Berkshire for similar vehicle checks.

Due to the delay it took to get an entry into the system all we could say, if there was no trace in the record, was 'Not reported stolen' as it could have been stolen and details had not reached Supplement F. Likewise, if the vehicle was shown as stolen, care had to be taken that it had not been recovered and the cancellation had not reached Supplement F.

Similar systems would have operated in other force control rooms.

I Remember When…

Memory of:
Personal memory.

When on M1 motorway patrol at Newport Pagnell in 1969 and 1970 we were faced with the problem of how to establish if a vehicle travelling on the M1 had recently been stolen. The system mentioned above was the only method available to our Control Room in Kidlington.

If a vehicle was travelling southbound and had been stolen from the Midlands area, a teleprinter message would not have been circulated to Thames Valley unless it was known it would come to the Thames Valley area. Therefore, the check had to rely on Supplement F and the possible ten-day delay.

What was available was the ability for a check to be made to the Regional Criminal Record Office where details of a recently stolen vehicle would have been circulated.

If the vehicle we were interested in was travelling south, or had an index number indicating it could have originated from the Midlands area, a check could be made of MidCRO (based in Birmingham) which covered the Midlands area. Or if it was thought the vehicle could have originated from the North East, a check would have been made with ManCRO (based in Manchester), and for the home counties it was NSYCRO.

This was the most effective method available to obtain information before we stopped a vehicle. We always had the problem where the vehicle may have been originally stolen from the Midlands but was travelling northbound with an index number originating from the southwest, and checks focused on NSYCRO failed to produce any information if the vehicle was stolen.

POLICE DUTIES

This was where you developed the 'gut feeling' from the behaviour of the driver and passengers.

Stolen Car Books

I Remember When...

Memories of:
Jamie Eves *(Joined Berkshire as a police cadet in 1965, appointed as a constable in 1966, retired in 1997 from Taplow Traffic)*
Personal Memory.

Jamie remembers during the early part of his service the need to maintain a personal stolen car book. These books were the same size as the Berkshire pocket book and details of stolen cars, given at the briefing at the start of the shift, or received during the shift, were entered into the book. This enabled the constable while on patrol, when discovering a motor vehicle that could have been stolen to do an initial check in his stolen car book. Prior to the introduction of personal radios, this was the only immediate method available to the foot or cycle patrol constable. When personal radios were introduced they could contact their station and ask for a vehicle check. The local radio controller at the police station would then phone the Force Control Room and the process I have outlined above was followed.

Obtaining details of ownership of a motor vehicle

I Remember When...

Memory of:
Dick Godfrey *(Joined Buckinghamshire in 1956, retired in 1986 from Newbury).*

Dick remembers that to obtain details of the owner of a motor vehicle, a buff coloured card called a RF 16/3 had to be completed and sent to the district or county council where the vehicle was originally registered.

POLICE DUTIES

This was identified through the last two letters in the index number e.g. KJB 72D was registered with Berkshire County Council, which had the letters RX, JB and JO.

Dick remembers that, in Buckinghamshire in the early 1960s, a constable had to submit a report as to the reason why the details of the owner of a car was required, and this had to be approved by the Officer in Charge of Divisional Administration before the RF16/3 was completed.

The whole process, from first identifying the need for the registered owner's details and acquiring the information via the post, could take several weeks.

I Remember When...

Memory of:
Personal memory.

Between 1963 and 1965 while a cadet in the Berkshire Control Room, there were many occasions when a request was made over the radio from a patrol to obtain details of the registered owner. This was only allowed for urgent requirements and only possible during the working hours of a council (Monday to Friday 9am-5pm). It entailed me first establishing, through the last two letters of the index number, the council to contact, and then telephoning the council, to explain the circumstances of the need. Once established that it was an urgent requirement, they would look up and provide the details. Outside of the normal working hours, the urgent requirement had to be approved by a senior officer as it required contacting the police force covering the council offices, and then calling out someone to go and open the offices and obtain the information.

I Remember When...

Memory of:
David Marchant *(Joined Thames Valley Police in 1973, retired in 2003 from Reading).*

POLICE DUTIES

David remembers that in 1973 when he was posted to Reading, part of his initial training was a visit to the Reading Borough Council Offices and being shown how to get details of a motor vehicle that was registered with them. On night duty, when there was an urgent requirement for registered owner's details, a constable would obtain the keys to the Council Offices from the police station, and go and look up the required details. Although a lot quicker than the postal enquiry, this could take several hours from the need being identified to the request being forwarded to Reading Police and the constable obtaining the information.

What happens now...

With the introduction of the Police National Computer (PNC) in 1974 immediate access was available to details of stolen vehicles. A vehicle check made on PNC will not only give details regarding if the vehicle is stolen or involved in crime, but details of ownership and confirmation of the make, model, colour and Vehicle Identification Number (VIN) and all this is immediately available.

One important development is the Automatic Number Plate Recognition System (ANPR). A camera records the index number of a vehicle as it passes, and automatically checks it against the ANPR database. Where a 'hit' occurs, this is immediately flagged up to the person monitoring the system.

ANPR cameras are positioned in various static locations, and also fitted to some police vehicles, especially Roads Policing vehicles. At the beginning of each patrol, the vehicle's database is updated so that information is up-to-date. When a 'hit' occurs, there are various alert signals, depending on the type of hit. The crew of the car will then determine what action to take.

The ANPR database not only links to PNC but other databases that can reveal offences and other information to provide 'hits' connected with insurance, vehicle testing, taxation and criminal use of the vehicle.

The ANPR system allows an ANPR equipped vehicle to drive around a car park and check each index number of the vehicles parked there. This is far more efficient than the constable walking around the car park checking numbers against those recorded in his stolen car book.

POLICE DUTIES

Motor vehicles and key points (or check points)

I Remember When...

Memory of:
Dick Allen *(Joined Berkshire as a boy clerk in 1948, at Newbury - later role changed to police cadet - following return from national service appointed as a constable in 1952, retired in 1984 from Banbury).*

Dick remembers, when a vehicle was reported stolen within Berkshire, the requirement to man Key Points. If a vehicle was stolen in Reading, Key Points were manned in East and West Berkshire. If the vehicle was stolen in the East of the county, Key Points were normally restricted to the East of the county, with a similar procedure for the West of the county. Key Points were at nominated locations on the main roads.

When Dick started at Ascot (1952), the Key Point was on the A329 junction with the A332 at Heatherwood Cross Roads (now Heatherwood Roundabout). If there were insufficient numbers of duty constables available or contactable from the duty shift, men from single quarters were required to turn out and man the Key Point.

During the hours of darkness, hurricane lamps were issued, because street lighting on many of the main roads outside of the towns did not exist. One other piece of equipment that had to be taken to a Key Point was a Bakelite 'grenade' shaped object which contained red paint, not explosives. The idea was that if the suspected stolen vehicle failed to stop, the grenade was thrown at the windscreen of the vehicle. The red paint would not only distort the vision of the driver, but also make the vehicle more readily identifiable.

What happens now...

Where a vehicle has been recently stolen, details will be broadcast to police vehicles in the area. Specified check points are not manned as we now have the Automatic Number Plate Recognition (ANPR) system. When a known stolen vehicle passes an ANPR camera and sets off an alert, details can be broadcast to police vehicles in the area, giving details of the location and the stolen vehicle's direction of travel.

Recording vehicles seen at night

I Remember When...

Memories of:
Geoff Allen *(Joined Reading Borough as a police cadet in 1957, appointed as a constable in 1959, retired in 1985 from Ascot)*
Ken Amery *(Joined Berkshire as a police cadet in 1964, appointed as a constable in 1966, retired in 1996 from Windsor)*
Dick Allen *(Joined Berkshire as a boy clerk in 1948, at Newbury - later role changed to police cadet - following return from national service appointed as a constable in 1952, retired in 1984 from Banbury)*
Jamie Eves *(Joined Berkshire as a police cadet in 1965, appointed as a constable in 1966, retired in 1997 from Taplow Traffic).*

All remember the requirement to record all vehicles seen between 0030 and 0530, as people out at this time could be involved in crime, or could be potential witnesses to crime occurring during the night. Log sheets had to be handed in at the end of the night shift and were then available to officers investigating overnight crime.

What happens now...

We now have Automatic Number Plate Recognition (ANPR). The logs of vehicles passing a particular camera can be referred to in the investigation of crime.

Early Police pedal cycle

POLICE DUTIES

Police Duties – cycle beats

I Remember When…

Memory of:
Dick Allen *(Joined Berkshire as a boy clerk in 1948, at Newbury - later role changed to police cadet - following return from national service appointed as a constable in 1952, retired in 1984 from Banbury).*

Dick remembers performing cycle beats at Ascot (1952). Conference Points would be designated to ensure maximum cover was provided for the area. With the total area covered by some rural section stations he felt that, on average, 15 miles could be expected to be covered before meal break and another 15 miles after meal break.

I Remember When…

Memory of:
Cameron Floate *(Joined Oxfordshire in 1951, retired in 1981 from Maidenhead).*

Cameron remembers when at Witney, between 1953 and 1955, his allocated conference points - which he had to cycle between - took him through Blenheim Park. This was to provide a police patrol in the park. When the park was closed, the officers would take a key to the gates, held at Witney Police Station, in order that they could pass through the park.

Cameron remembers when initially posted to the rural beat at Wargrave, all his duties were performed on a bicycle. This included cycling from Wargrave to Wokingham to attend the Magistrates Court.

He also remembers on one occasion he was on a Conference Point in Crazies Hill, Wargrave, when he received a telephone call to attend a traffic accident on the adjoining rural beat at Beenhams Heath, Shurlock Row. This was a distance of nearly seven miles. When he arrived, the parties involved were still there!

Cameron was later issued with a motorcycle, equipped with a police radio, which meant that the need to make conference points as a means of contact with the police station no longer existed. His bicycle also became redundant, only used when his motorcycle was not available.

POLICE DUTIES

I Remember When...

Memory of:
Mike Edwards *(Joined Buckinghamshire in 1952, retired in 1982 from Aylesbury).*

Mike remembers performing cycle patrols when stationed at Colnbrook. Langley had not been developed and the police station for the area was based in Sutton Lane, Colnbrook. Conference Points were set at hourly intervals and could be as far apart as George Green and Wraysbury.

Like many officers who have referred to Conference Points, he remembers often being met by the duty Sergeant or Inspector, who would drive to the point to check that the constable was making the point and to sign the constable's pocket book. When it was wet or cold, the comment is often made that the Sergeant or Inspector would remain in the car and the pocket book was passed through the window for signing.

What happens now...

With the introduction of radios in police vehicles in the 1950's and rural constables being issued with motorcycles, the need for cycle beats reduced. With the introduction of personal radios, enabling contact to be maintained with patrolling police officers, the need for Conference Points no longer existed. Cycles are still used by some members of Community Teams when patrolling their areas.

Cycles are still used to patrol neighbourhoods

POLICE DUTIES

Patrolling the beat

I Remember When...

Memories of:
Ken Amery *(Joined Berkshire as a police cadet in 1964, appointed as a constable in 1966, retired in 1996 from Windsor)*
Jamie Eves *(Joined Berkshire as a police cadet in 1965, appointed as a constable in 1966, retired in 1997 from Taplow, Traffic)*
Geoff Allen *(Joined Reading Borough as a police cadet in 1957, appointed as a constable in 1959, retired in 1985 from Ascot)*
Jack Penny *(Joined Reading Borough in 1951, retired in 1983 from Reading Traffic)*
Personal Memory.

All remember various aspects of patrolling the beat. Knowledge of the beat, the properties, the roads, the back alleys and the people was a very important part of 'beat craft', and there was a pride taken in working the beat.

On night duty, commercial property was checked for security both by 'shaking the door handles' and also checking the backs of the properties. Access via fire escape ladders could give you, and potential burglars, movement from one street to another. Vacant property was checked for people sleeping rough.

Jamie remembers that, during the day, truncheon straps had to be out of sight but at night they could be visible for ease of drawing the truncheon if required. **I** remember that the principle was that during the day whilst on foot patrol the aim was to be conspicuous, for example, by walking on the outside of the pavement. When it was dark, the aim was reversed and you tried to be inconspicuous, by keeping to the shadows and the inside of the pavement. To assist this our night helmets had black helmet plates. By being inconspicuous aided the detection of the person committing an offence, and also developed the feeling that you never knew when a policeman may appear!

Once allocated to a beat you had to be out patrolling it as soon as possible. Time in the police station had to be authorised. A return to the police station was only at scheduled meal breaks, or with a prisoner. Even if it was wet or very cold you remained on your beat.

POLICE DUTIES

Geoff and Jack can remember that if you were caught by the Sergeant having an unauthorised cup of tea, you would be disciplined. Sergeants were also out patrolling, but their role was to make sure that the constables were correctly patrolling their beats. We all remember being checked by the duty Sergeant or Inspector at our schedule conference points. Pocket books were checked and signed to confirm their inspection.

Geoff and Jack both remember how beats had to be worked in Reading Borough. When shops and other commercial property were closed, it was the responsibility of the patrolling police constable to check the security of premises at the front and any other accessible parts.

The checking of the front of the property was often referred to as 'Shaking door handles'. As constables walked down a street, they would try the front door handles to check if each shop was secure. In Reading there were two arcades which had security gates at the entrance. On night duty the constables allocated to the beat on which the arcades were located had to collect a key from the police station, open the security gates, and physically check the property within the arcade.

Property would be checked several times during the shift. Should a shop breaking occur on a beat that was not discovered by the patrolling constable, they would be required to account for the times they checked the property and why they had not discovered that the premises had been broken into.

It was not uncommon for some constables to carry a role of black cotton with them on nights. This was used to string across a passageway or alleyway that gave access to the rear of some properties. Once the property had been checked for the first time, the cotton was put in place. On subsequent visits, if the cotton was still in place it could be assumed that access had not been made to the passageway and the security of the property was still intact. This was all part of learning 'beat craft' which also included walking down any one-way street facing the oncoming traffic, so you could see what vehicles were approaching, not when they had gone past.

Geoff remembers that a record had to be kept of all motor vehicles seen after midnight and this record had to be handed in at the end of the shift. In addition it was expected that all people seen at night would be stopped and spoken to and their details obtained. The 'persons seen at night' form was also handed in at the end of the shift.

Geoff remembers that effectively a zero tolerance approach operated in Reading. If a person was drunk and was either disorderly or incapable, they were arrested. If a group of people assembled and were obstructing a pavement and refused to move on, they were arrested.

POLICE DUTIES

If a person was found sleeping rough, their details were obtained and checked against a 'Persons Sleeping Rough' book at the police station. If the person's name was already in the book, indicating that they had already received a warning about sleeping rough, they were arrested.

On Saturday nights and at certain other times, constables were deployed to special points, at or close to certain public houses or cross roads where they could observe several public houses. This was to monitor the time the premises were closing and the state of persons leaving the premises and give advice when necessary. Where advice was not taken and trouble could be anticipated, arrests were made.

Geoff and Jack both remember that handcuffs were not issued to Reading Borough Officers and, due to the lack of communication with the police station when you arrested a person while on the beat, the prisoner had to be placed in a 'police hold' and walked back to the police station.

Geoff particularly remembers the arrest of one violent drunk in Kings Road, Reading near the junction with Orts Road. Unable to summon any assistance, he had to place the man in the required police hold and struggle with him back to the police station. He states that, on arrival, he was somewhat short of breath and it took some time to recount the details of the arrest to the duty sergeant.

Jack remembers a similar incident when on one late evening he arrested a person for drunk and disorderly in Wokingham Road, Reading, near the Three Tuns Cross Roads. This was more than two miles from the police station. If it had been in the town centre it was normal to walk the prisoner back to the police station, but two miles was too far, especially with a drunk and disorderly.

A Thames Valley bus was passing enroute to Reading Railway Station. Jack stopped the bus and asked the driver if he could assist. The driver was even more helpful than Jack had anticipated as he changed his route as he approached the railway station and stopped at the police station.
– *No fare was required.*

No handcuffs - use approved police hold to secure and move prisoner

85

POLICE DUTIES

Police duties – Animals

Dealing with animals – Stray dogs

I Remember When...

Memory of:
Personal memory.

I remember when stray dogs were the responsibility of the police. Stray dogs would be handed in at police stations, and persons missing their dogs would make enquiries at their police station. Details of stray dogs were entered into a stray dog register. Dogs had to be retained in police possession for seven days before they could be handed to a dog rescue organisation. Each police station had a set of stray dog kennels and it was the responsibility of the constable performing station duties to feed any stray dogs in the kennels and keep the kennels clean. Where the station had a police cadet, this was a responsibility delegated to them.

I remember that when living in the police house attached to Twyford Police Station, the barking created by some stray dogs while in the kennels was a problem for my wife and I, and local residents. This was solved by bringing the dogs into the house at night and taking them for walks. Where the dogs were noisy during the day, my wife would sometimes walk the dogs to work with her and, with human contact, the dogs were well behaved and quiet.

What happens now...

Stray dogs are now the responsibility of the local council, and their dog wardens. Stray dogs are no longer a direct responsibility of the police service.

POLICE DUTIES

Livestock market and movement licences

I Remember When...

Memories of:
Geoff Allen *(joined Reading Borough in 1957 as a police Cadet, appointed as a constable in 1959, retired in 1985 from Ascot)*
Personal memory.

Geoff remembers that a Sergeant attended each livestock market in Reading for the purposes of issuing swine movement licences. As a constable he remembers visiting a small holding to check that a pig, recently purchased from a livestock market, was kept isolated from other pigs for a specified number of days.

I can remember a similar role completed by a senior constable at the Bracknell Market and, as a constable at Twyford, receiving copies of issued movement licences and visiting and checking pigs on a small holding at Twyford.

What happens now...

The issue of pig movement licences and checking that licence requirements are being complied with is now the responsibility of the Department for Environment Food and Rural Affairs (Defra) and their inspectors. The police service is no longer directly involved with agricultural animals and will only become involved when called upon by Defra when there is a major outbreak of a notifiable disease, such as Foot and Mouth.

POLICE DUTIES

Police Duties - Civil Defence – Early Warning Systems

Following World War Two, the Cold War developed, and there was a threat of nuclear attack. Civil Defence was a role included in police duties, and training. Some memories linked to this are given below:

I Remember When...

Memories of:
Dick Jenkinson (Joined Thames Valley as a police cadet in 1970, appointed as a constable in 1971, retired in 2001 from Amersham)
Malcolm Walker (Joined Berkshire as a police cadet in 1967, appointed as a constable in 1970, retired in 1999 from Aylesbury Crown Court Liaison).

Dick and Malcolm both remember the early warning system that was in each police station. This was a box which when turned on would emit a beeping noise. On a regular basis, written notification of a test were sent out. On these occasions, each box had to be switched on and monitored. When the test warning was sent the beeping turned to a high pitched warbling noise, followed by a verbal message and a code word that had to be entered onto the notification form that had to be completed and returned.

What happens now...

The early warning system was part of the civil defence planning and procedures that were present when there was a threat of nuclear attack as a result of the Cold War. Civil defence was the plan for protection of citizens of the country. The Cold War no longer exists and the early warning process is no longer in place.

Civil defence, which was focused on a nuclear attack, is now focused on planning regarding terrorist attacks and other major incidents that could occur, e.g. major disasters, plane or train crashes. The police service is involved in the prevention of terrorist incidents, and with local authorities and the other emergency services in planning for the prevention of major incidents and what should be done if one occurs.

POLICE DUTIES

Police duties – Notification of unoccupied property

I Remember When…

Memories of:
Jamie Eves *(Joined Berkshire as a police cadet in 1965, appointed as a constable in 1966, retired in 1997 from Taplow Traffic)*
Dick Jenkinson *(Joined Thames Valley as a police cadet in 1970, appointed as a constable in 1971, retired in 2001 from Amersham)*
Steve Evans *(Joined Thames Valley in 1975, retired in 2005 from National Crime Squad)*
Dick Godfrey *(Joined Buckinghamshire in 1956, retired in 1986 from Newbury)*
Personal memory.

All can remember the system which encouraged members of the public to notify their local police station when they would be away and their property was going to be unoccupied. This was done on an understanding that the property would be checked by a police officer while they were away.

All can remember the allocation of unoccupied property forms when starting a patrol and the requirement to check the property.

My memory of checking a particular property is recorded under ***Police Cadets – Duties at Woodley.***

Although this was a system that appears to have been carried out in all police forces as a crime prevention initiative, I am not sure what percentage of checks revealed whether the premises had been broken into.

What happens now…

No similar scheme still exists, although prevention of crime is still a very important priority.
People are encouraged to join Neighbourhood Watch schemes, and when their property is empty, to ensure that their local neighbours know so they can keep an eye on it.

POLICE DUTIES

Police duties – Maintenance of key holders registers

I Remember When...

Memories of:
Dick Jenkinson *(Joined Thames Valley as a police cadet in 1970, appointed as a constable in 1971, retired in 2001 from Amersham)*
Personal Memory.

Dick and I can both remember the time-consuming administration task of maintaining key holders registers. With the regular patrol duty of checking property for insecurities it was not uncommon to find them. It would then be necessary to contact the key holder to come and secure the property.

Burglar alarms were another need for key holders. Alarms would often be activated. I can remember there being three types of alarms: The alarm that was activated on the premises, the alarm that was directly connected to the local police station and, with the development of technology, the alarm that when activated, was notified to the local police station via the 999 system. Both the 999 and directly-connected alarms could have a delay built into them that only rang the alarms on the premises after a number of minutes, giving time for police to respond to the initial notification.

Whichever system when an alarm was activated the property had to be checked and the alarm reset.

Problems were encountered when insecurities were found and the notified key holders had changed, or the ownership of the property had changed and the amended details not provided to maintain police records. It was therefore necessary, at regular intervals, to check details held on the key holder cards to ensure that they were up-to-date.

What happens now...

Alarm systems are managed by the alarm companies. Police will respond to alarm activations, but the alarm companies are responsible for the maintenance of their key holder details.

Police duties – Major events

Selection of officers for duty at the event

I Remember When...

Memory of:
Dick Allen *(Joined Berkshire as a boy clerk in 1948, at Newbury - later role changed to police cadet - following return from national service appointed as a constable in 1952, retired in 1984 from Banbury).*

Dick remembers that as the Admin Sergeant based in the Berkshire Headquarters at Sulhamstead he was involved in preparing the police operation order for the two major events that occurred on an annual basis in Berkshire - Royal Ascot Races and Henley Royal Regatta. His role was to allocate named officers to each of the duties identified in the operation order.

Dick remembers that all leave was cancelled for the duration of Royal Ascot Races as one third of the Berkshire Force were required to police Ascot, leaving two thirds for policing the county.

Where an officer had attended the previous Ascot and had performed their duty well, they were automatically allocated the same duty in the next year's order, and this part of the order was relatively simple to complete.

Where a replacement was required, for example if the officer had retired, or had been deemed not suitable for a duty at Ascot, Dick had to identify a list of potential replacements which he then had to take to the Deputy Chief Constable, who would personally select a suitable replacement.

What happens now...

Policing arrangements for a major event are normally the reponsibility of the Local Police Area (LPA) where the event is taking place.

POLICE DUTIES

In recent years, any policing required for inside the event will be at the cost of the organisers and more and more organisers are using specially-trained stewards rather than police officers.

Where police are required, they would be supplied by the LPA, and if additional police officers were required they would be supplied by surrounding LPAs, but at a charge as each LPA commander has a budget responsibility regarding manpower costs.

In the cases of special major events, such as Royal Ascot Races or policing of the Olympics, the planning is Headquarters-based. Manpower for the policing requirement would come from LPAs and funded from Headquarters-held budgets.

Provision of catering for police officers at Royal Ascot Races

I Remember When...

Memories of:
Dick Allen *(Joined Berkshire as a boy clerk in 1948, at Newbury - later role changed to police cadet - following return from national service appointed as a constable in 1952, retired in 1984 from Banbury)*
Ken Amery *(Joined Berkshire as a police cadet in 1964, appointed as a constable in 1966, retired in 1996 from Windsor)*
Personal memory.

Dick remembers that the policing operation at Ascot Races was based in a building that had originally been built as barracks for the Metropolitan Police officers who policed Royal Ascot Races prior to the Berkshire Constabulary taking over the responsibility.

Police officers attending the event worked long hours *(See entry under hours of duty)* and while they were at Ascot they had to be provided with suitable refreshments. This included a morning refreshment, lunch, afternoon refreshment, plus the regular provision of cups of tea. The preparing, cooking and supply of the refreshments was the responsibility of a group of constables under the supervision of an Inspector.

This was a regular team, consisting mostly of the more elderly constables who had performed the role over several years. The Inspector had overall responsibility for ordering the required food and ensuring that the necessary equipment was installed prior to the start of the event. All these officers were billeted in the dormitory at the police station.

POLICE DUTIES

Dick remembers that all of the vegetables used were grown in the walled vegetable garden that was part of Sulhamstead House, the Berkshire Constabulary Headquarters. The gardens and grounds of Sulhamstead were maintained by gardeners employed by the Berkshire Constabulary.

Ken remembers that as a police cadet he performed duties at Royal Ascot Races, assisting in the provision of the catering to police officers. *(See entry under police cadet duties).*

We all remember that each officer performing duty at Ascot Races was issued with vouchers showing their refreshment entitlement. A voucher had to be handed in as payment for the refreshment.

The vouchers covered morning refreshment, lunch, afternoon refreshment, and six cups of tea.

Dependant upon their duties and their personal needs, many officers did not use all of their vouchers. At the end of the day, the spare vouchers could be used to purchase chocolates and sweets from the snack bar and be taken home. Many families looked forward to Royal Ascot Races.

What happens now...

Where catering is required at a major event there is a mobile catering unit, based at Headquarters, staffed by civilian employees. This can be deployed to the planned major event or any unplanned major incident. Stocks for use by the catering team come from commercial suppliers.

Police duties – Station based duties

I Remember When...

Memory of:
Cyril Wise *(Joined Buckinghamshire in 1947, retired in 1965 from Aylesbury Traffic).*

Cyril remembers that in his early service when stationed at Bletchley, there was a requirement for one constable to remain in the police station, 24 hours a day. At the time there was only a voluntary fire brigade covering the Bletchley area and if the fire brigade was required it was the constable in the police station who operated the call out system.

POLICE DUTIES

Note: The separate Fire and Rescue Service did not come into effect until 1948. Prior to the Second World War (1939-1945) any fire response cover was the responsibility of the Local Borough, City or County Council. At the start of the war, the fire service was placed on a national footing, returning to local authority control after the war. Although some boroughs and cities had a paid fire service, many county towns had to rely on volunteers to man the provided fire equipment. Often, especially in the boroughs and cities with a paid fire service, the Chief Constable was also the Senior Fire Officer. Many of the local fire services were based on volunteers and prior to the separate Fire and Rescue Service coming into effect, patrolling police officers were also involved in responding to fire calls.

What happens now...

Buckinghamshire Fire and Rescue service started in 1948 when all responsibility for call outs transferred to the Fire Service, although today some areas still rely on volunteer (retained) firemen to man the appliances.

Buckinghamshire Constabulary helmet plate

POLICE DUTIES

Maintaining the police station heating system

I Remember When…

Memory of:
Cameron Floate *(Joined Oxfordshire in 1951, transferred to Berkshire in 1956, retired in 1981 from Maidenhead).*

Cameron, remembers that when at Banbury (1951), it was the responsibility of the night station constable to ensure that the station boiler was stoked and working. The boiler served the police station, single quarters and adjoining court room. He remembers on at least one occasion the boiler had not been stoked and went out, resulting in a cold police station and court room. Needless to say, the Superintendent and Magistrates were not happy with this 'neglect of police duty'.

I Remember When…

Memory of:
Ken Wells *(joined Metropolitan Police in 1962, transferred to Berkshire in 1965, retired in 1993 from Scenes of Crime Department, Bracknell).*

Ken remembers that when he was at Wokingham it was the responsibility of the constable performing early turn station duty to light the fire in the Chief Inspector's Office and CID Office.

A fire was maintained 24 hours a day in the front office and for ease a shovelful of hot coals was taken from this fire and carried, through the station and up a flight of stairs to the Chief Inspector's Office and another to the CID Office.

Ken remembers that on one occasion when he was performing the task, a hot coal fell off the shovel and burnt a hole in the lino floor in the Chief Inspector's Office. With the aid of the Duty Sergeant, who had permitted the method of lighting the fire, the damage was concealed by slightly moving the rug and desk in the office, and was never noticed by the Chief Inspector.

POLICE DUTIES

What happens now...

It is obvious that health and safety was not applied as legislation requires today. However, modern heating systems are either gas or oiled fired and there is no need for police officers to be involved in maintaining them.

Duties of 'Houseman'

I Remember When...

Memory of:
Geoff Allen *(joined Reading Borough in 1957 as a police cadet, appointed as a constable in 1959, retired in 1985 from Ascot).*

Geoff remembers that when he first joined Reading Borough as a constable on each shift one constable was assigned to the duties of 'Houseman'.

Duties of the 'Houseman' included - in addition to general station duties - keeping the coke boiler fully stoked and visiting and feeding the stray dogs. The dogs were kept in kennels in the Cattle Market about half a mile from the police station. When there were no canteen staff on duty, especially on night shift, the Houseman's duties also included making tea for constables on meal break, and cooking items that they provided for their meal breaks.

This was a coveted duty, especially by the more elderly constables, as mostly it was a duty performed in the dry and warm.

Cleaning the police station

I Remember When...

Memory of:
John Harker *(Joined Oxfordshire as a police cadet in 1958, appointed as a constable in 1961, retired in 1987 from District Police Training Centre, Cwmbran).*

POLICE DUTIES

John remembers that the duties of the early turn constable on the Kidlington Section was to sweep and polish the floor of the Kidlington Section Station, as no cleaner was provided.

The station was attached to the side of the Sergeant's house and their reward for polishing the floor was sometimes a visit by the Sergeant, coming through the connecting door from his house with a cup of tea.

What happens now...

Police stations have rooms where officers can take their meal breaks.
A microwave and kettle are also provided for use.
There is access to a sink, and cutlery is provided on the understanding that the people who use it should wash up.
The role of a police officer is focused on police duties outside of the station. Although an obvious responsibility not to make a mess when in the police station, and wash up cups, there are cleaners employed for cleaning duties at police stations.

Police duties – Sudden Deaths

I Remember When...

Memories of:
Cyril Wise *(joined Buckinghamshire in 1947, retired in 1975 from Aylesbury Traffic)*
Ken Amery *(joined Berkshire as a police cadet in 1964, appointed as a constable in 1966, retired in 1996 from Windsor)*
Personal memory.

Cyril remembers an allowance that could be claimed from the Coroner when you dealt with a sudden death and had to accompany the body to the mortuary and prepare it for identification by a relative. For a normal sudden death the allowance was ten shillings (50p), but for a badly injured or decomposed body one pound (£1) could be claimed.

POLICE DUTIES

Ken and I can remember this being available in Berkshire. It should be mentioned that at this time there were no separate officers working as Coroner's Officers. If you were sent to a sudden death you were required to see the whole process through. In most cases, mortuaries were not part of a hospital, but often single-brick buildings maintained by the local council.

Where the death was not suspicious, the process would include

- seeing the body into the mortuary

- preparing the body for formal identification by a relative

- arranging the identification

- arranging the post mortum

- carrying out a full investigation as to the circumstances of the death

- obtaining the necessary statements and submitting a full report to the Coroner.

If the Coroner decided that an inquest was required, then arranging the inquest and being present at the inquest.

Where the death was suspicious then the investigation would be the responsibility of a Senior CID Officer.

What happens now...

Although police officers still attend sudden deaths, when the body is removed from the scene it will go to a mortuary, which is part of a hospital, where hospital staff deal. Unless the death is suspicious and subject to a CID investigation, civilian Coroner's Officers will deal with all the subsequent actions regarding identification and preparing the necessary sudden death file for the Coroner. If an inquest is required this will be arranged by the Coroner's Officers. No allowances are paid to police officers for attending a sudden death.

Police Housing

Free police housing and a good pension scheme – not the pay – were two of the incentives to join the police service before the late 1970s.

For single police officers, accommodation was provided either in single quarters, often attached to a police station, or lodgings were found and paid for. For married officers, a police house was provided. In county police forces, these could be attached to a police station or a rural beat house in a village, with a police office attached or in some cases built in a group, forming a police community. In Oxford City and Reading Borough, although some houses were provided, many officers lived in their own houses, for which a housing allowance was paid.

With the free police housing, especially the rural beat houses, also came some advantages and disadvantages as will be seen from the below memories.

I Remember When…

Memories of:
Rodney Watson *(Joined Berkshire in 1964 as a police cadet, appointed as a constable in 1965, retired in 1995 from Taplow Traffic)*
Personal memory.

Rodney and I both remember that when we joined the Berkshire Constabulary in the 1960s, a police officer either had to live in police provided accommodation or, if single and no single quarters were available, you could find your own lodgings but these had to be visited by a senior officer and approved suitable for occupation by a police officer. Lodgings in a public house were not suitable!

In a county force you were not allowed to buy your own house, and I remember an officer who on joining sold his house and was provided with a police house.

Officers in Reading Borough and Oxford City were allowed to live in their own houses, for which a rent allowance was paid. Shortly after amalgamation the situation was rationalised, and officers throughout Thames Valley were permitted to live in their own house and a housing allowance was paid.

POLICE HOUSING

What happens now...

Following the Sheehy Report of 1993, the provision of police accommodation or the paying of a housing allowance was stopped for police officers joining the police service. Officers already in the police force and in receipt of a rent allowance had the allowance frozen at the rate they were receiving.
  Where a newly-joined police officer was allowed to occupy a vacant police single quarter or a police-owned house that could not be sold, they were charged a rent for living in the property.

Requirement to live within 20 miles of your station

I Remember When...

Memory of:
Personal memory.

I remember that as a policeman you were required to live in a police house in the area that you were posted. When the right to own your own property was fully introduced in Thames Valley Police, the requirement to live within the area was defined as within 20 miles of the station you were posted to.

In 1976 I was living in my own house at Slough, when I was promoted and posted to Reading. As I was residing 21.2 miles from Reading, I was required to move and live within 20 miles of Reading Police Station. This had to be achieved within six months. A removal allowance was given and, to assist, if a police house was vacant within the required 20 miles, you were allowed to move into it on a temporary basis while the sale of one house and the purchase of another was completed.

POLICE HOUSING

What happens now...

The requirement to live within 20 miles still exists. However, moves are normally planned to enable an officer to remain within the 20 miles.
If the officer has to move to meet the 20-mile requirement they can claim a removal allowance. However, officers can sign a withdrawal from the 20 mile requirement which, once signed, applies for the remainder of their service. Officers frequently travel from outside the 20-mile radius to attend their duty station.

Discovering that provision of a police house did not apply to women police officers with children (Situation changed by 1977)

I Remember When...

Memory of:
Barbara Marchant *(Joined Thames Valley in 1975, retired in 2005 from Reading).*

Barbara remembers that when she joined in 1975, she was a single mother with three children, however the allocation of police houses only applied to male officers. It was not until 1977, after she had completed her probation and was confirmed in her position of a constable, that a police house was allocated to her.

What happens now...

The situation explained by Barbara ceased in 1977, and police accommodation was available for female officers on the same basis as male officers. With the recommendations of the 1993 Sheehy report being implemented, this removed the right for provision of free accommodation from all officers joining the police service, therefore the above situation would not arise today.

POLICE HOUSING

Living in single quarters

I Remember When…

Memory of:
Dick Allen *(Joined Berkshire as a boy clerk in 1948 at Newbury - later role changed to police cadet - following return from national service appointed as a constable in 1952, retired in 1984 from Banbury).*

Dick remembers after initial training (1952) he was posted to single quarters at Ascot. He remembers six poorly-equipped bedrooms and an old dining room/lounge situated adjacent to an antiquated kitchen. There was a cook employed to cook weekday breakfast and lunch for single officers using food paid for by the single officers. At all other times, officers had to cook their own meals - a role that they often shared. In 1952, rationing was still in force and many of the single men had previous military service.

In addition to a cook, a cleaner was also employed to clean the police station and the single quarters.

As single men in single quarters, they were subject to many restrictions based on the fact that as an occupant of police single quarters you were answerable to police regulations and requirements at all times while in occupancy.

Dick remembers that as a single man you were not allowed to leave single quarters unless you booked out in a register and provided a contact telephone number.

He also remembers that when he first started at Ascot, if a car was stolen in Berkshire and it could be anticipated that it may come through Ascot, a key point (also known as a check point) had to be manned at the junction of the A329 and A332 (now Heatherwood Roundabout). If there were insufficient officers on duty and immediately unavailable, off duty constables from single quarters were required to man the check point. No overtime compensation was paid. *See Police Duties – Motor Vehicles and Key Points.*

POLICE HOUSING

Dick also remembers that not only were single men a ready source of manpower to man key points, they were a ready source for changes of duty. He states that it was not unknown when working a series of day duties, enabling social activities in the evening, to return to single quarters to find a note on your pillow informing you that your duty for the following day had been changed from a day shift to an evening duty. No compensation was payable and social life was affected.

I Remember When...

Memory of:
Cameron Floate *(Joined Oxfordshire in 1951, retired in 1981 from Maidenhead).*

Cameron remembers, when he started at Banbury, residing in one of three single quarters at the station. He remembers he had the smallest room, which was unheated and did not have any electric points other than the central ceiling lamp.

What happens now...

Few police officers live in the previously designated 'single quarters'. It is only where these single quarters are part of a police building that they remain in police ownership. Many of these single quarters have been converted into offices, but where they still remain as single quarters the occupants have to pay a rent for them.

The rooms have to be maintained at a suitable standard to comply with legislation relating to rented property.

Living in police houses

I Remember When...

Memory of:
Cameron Floate *(Joined in Oxfordshire 1951, retired in 1981 from Maidenhead).*

103

POLICE HOUSING

Cameron recalls that when he first married, due to a shortage of police houses in Oxfordshire, he and his wife first had to share a police house with another married couple. He later found a farmhouse that was approved for police occupation, but again he had to move when the farmer required the farmhouse for farm staff.

It was at this point that he decided to transfer to Berkshire Constabulary and was allocated a rural beat house at Wargrave.

What happens now...

This would not occur today as officers have to find their own accommodation and pay for it themselves.

Oxford City Police helmet plate

POLICE HOUSING

Annual housing inspections

I Remember When...

Memories of:
Cameron Floate *(Joined in Oxfordshire 1951, retired in 1981 from Maidenhead)*
Rodney Watson *(Joined Berkshire in 1964 as a police cadet, appointed as a constable in 1965, retired in 1995 from Taplow Traffic)*
Personal memory.

I, together with Cameron, Rodney, and many others, remember the annual housing inspections that occurred in Berkshire Constabulary. The inspection was carried out by the Divisional Superintendent, accompanied by the County Architect.

The Superintendent ensured that the police house, gardens and any allocated equipment was being kept in good order. The County Architect was there to inspect the maintenance of the property and agree, subject to budgets, what decoration could be undertaken for the following year and what alterations may be possible. Redecoration was based on an internal redecoration every five years and an external painting every seven years.

It should be pointed out that although agreed to at the housing inspection, not all maintenance requests were met in the year, and a similar request was made the following year. One frequent request was for an increase in the number of electric points in the kitchen, especially by occupants of older police houses where often there was only one.

Where the occupant agreed to decorate internal rooms, a set allowance was provided for paint, paper and decorating materials. These had to be purchased from a nominated retailer. I remember the wallpaper selection was always from the back of the wallpaper book, where the cheaper papers could be found!

Equipment provided with a police house

I Remember When...

Memory of:
Dick Allen *Joined Berkshire as a boy clerk in 1948 at Newbury - later role changed to police cadet - following return from national service appointed as a constable in 1952, retired in 1984 from Banbury).*

POLICE HOUSING

Dick remembers that with each police house came an electric or gas cooker. When officers moved out of a police house, the house and gardens were inspected by a senior officer to ensure that they were being left suitable for occupation by the next officer who moved in.

Dick recalls that cookers could be a problem, particularly when the house you moved into had a clean but old cooker, and you had just left a house with a new, clean cooker. **Dick** also remembers that it was not uncommon for one person to move out in the morning and the next occupant to move in in the afternoon. He remembers that on one move he agreed with the incoming occupant to leave the coal fire boiler stoked so that the new occupant had hot water.

Removal allowance

I Remember When...

Memory of:
Dick Allen *Joined Berkshire as a boy clerk in 1948 at Newbury - later role changed to police cadet - following return from national service appointed as a constable in 1952, retired in 1984 from Banbury)*
Personal memory.

When you were required to move as part of your career in the police force, both a financial allowance and time allowance was given. The financial allowance was not large, but assisted in covering some of the cost for new curtains, carpets and rugs. The actual cost of the move by a removal company was paid for by the police.

The time off allowance was one day to prepare for the move, one day for the move, and one day to unpack and settle into the new house.

In my first ten years of married life, my wife and I moved five times. The moves were connected with postings to and within Traffic Department, and promotion. I remember that when we first chose carpeting it was a cord carpet that could be added to as we moved house. In our fourth house, when I completed laying the carpet in the lounge there was carpet from three previous houses plus a new piece. Thankfully, the carpet held its colour and it matched very well.

Curtains were another item that moved around, not only in your house. My first police house was in Twyford, Berkshire and I then moved to Bletchley. By coincidence, when my brother married, he was posted to the house that I had occupied in Twyford so we were able to assist him with curtains that fitted - *at no charge!*

POLICE HOUSING

Living in a rural beat house – additional duties

I Remember When...

Memories of:
Arthur Chaplin *(Joined Berkshire in 1949, retired in 1984 from Newbury)*
Cameron Floate *(Joined Oxfordshire in 1951, transferred to Berkshire in 1956, retired in 1981 from Maidenhead)*
George Brown *(Joined Berkshire in 1954, retired in 1984 from HQ Operations)*.

All remember living in rural police houses. In addition to performing split shifts (See *Police Duties – split shifts*), effectively you were never off duty as you were required to answer callers at the house, both telephone and personal callers. When you were away from the house working, this role fell to your wife.

Living in police houses on small sector stations – additional duties

I Remember When...

Memory of:
Dick Allen *(Joined Berkshire as a boy clerk in 1948 at Newbury - later role changed to police cadet - following return from national service appointed as a constable in 1952, retired in 1984 from Banbury)*
Personal memory.

Both Dick and I can remember the additional roles that came with living in police houses attached to small section stations.

Dick, in the late 1950s, was posted to a house adjoining the section station at Bracknell (before the development of Bracknell). The section performed duties between 0800 and 0200, with the police station being manned from 0800-2400. After 2400 the telephone was connected to one of two police houses, with the responsibility logged on the duty sheet. When you were nominated to receive calls you required to be at home. Between 2400 and 0200 if a call required the attendance of a police officer, you could contact the divisional station at Wokingham who would contact a patrolling police officer on their next conference point.

POLICE HOUSING

After 0200 if a police officer was required to attend, you had to get up and attend yourself. No additional pay was received for this duty even when there was a requirement to attend yourself.

I can remember a similar situation when I went to Twyford in 1966. Here, the telephone duty was covered by four officers. The police office was not manned every evening and the telephone was transferred to the police houses from 2000. Due to the introduction of radios in police vehicles, it was easier to contact patrolling officers and, after 0200, cover for the section was provided from Woodley, although there was the occasional need to turn out.

I also remember an additional role that my wife and I took on relating to stray dogs – see the entry under ***Police Duties – Dealing with Animals – Stray Dogs.***

What happens now…

As officers are no longer provided with police accommodation, once at home they are 'off duty'. Some officers perform duties which require them to be 'on call'. With modern communication systems this does not mean, when they are 'on call', that they are restricted to their house but the must be available to immediately attend their station and in a suitable state for duty – no drinking of alcohol whilst 'on call'.

Rural police house

Aide-memoires

I Remember When...

Memory of:
John Kearns *(Joined Thames Valley in 1970, retired in 2000 from Bracknell).*

John remembers a particular aide-memoroire that was issued by the Metropolitan Police to assist in the preparation of a form giving the description of a wanted or suspected person or one that had been arrested for a criminal offence. These forms were referred to as CRO 73 and CRO 74.

The Metropolitan Police was responsible for the central Criminal Record Office *(CRO)* which was based in New Scotland Yard, and it was to CRO that the CRO 73/74 was submitted. The aide-memoire *(pictured right)* was designed to try and bring a consistency to the descriptions used under various headings.

There were 26 headings and the aid-memoire had an accompanying aid chart that in sketch form, showed six different types of eyebrows, eight different styles of noses, three styles of ears, and four styles of ear lobes.

In addition to the elements of physical description, guidance was also given concerning unusual features, including mannerisms e.g. 'accomplishments (plays piano or other instrument, performs conjuring tricks or acrobatic feats), smokes (if a pipe, shape or make, gold or silver band, brand of tobacco: if cigarettes, brand, chain-smoker, makes own, peculiar manner of holding it); drinks beer, wine or spirits – favourite brand; associates with prostitutes; takes snuff.

The above will give an indication of the detail that was required for a well-completed descriptive form, although **John** did not come across many offenders that admitted to taking snuff!

DESCRIPTIONS

The "Descriptive Aid Chart" is not only for guidance of officers completing Forms C.R.O./73 and 74, but also to assist all officers in describing suspects, persons wanted, etc. Wherever possible, the description should be written down while it is fresh in the memory, e.g., when persons committing crimes have been seen but it has not been possible to arrest them or prevent their escape.

The following features should be noted wherever possible on the lines indicated:—

HEIGHT: Exact, if known, otherwise approximate; looks taller or shorter.

COMPLEXION: Fresh, ruddy, florid, pale, fair, sallow, blotchy, pimply, uses cosmetics.

HAIR: Colour, turning grey, going bald, wavy, permanent waved, straight, curly, frizzy, parted, unparted, brushed back, long, short, how cut, greased, unkempt, wears wig, bleached, dyed.

HEAD: Large, small, narrow, square.

EYEBROWS: As in item 1 on Chart.

NOSE: As in item 2 on Chart.

LIPS: As in item 3 on Chart.

CHIN: As in item 4 on Chart.

HANDS: Long, short, broad, long fingers, short fingers, well kept, rough; nails—long, short, bitten, dirty, manicured, varnished (colour).

MARKS: (especially those visible or on forearms—commence at top of head and work downwards): Scars, birthmarks, moles, freckles, tattoos, deformities, amputations, limp.

UNUSUAL FEATURES: Mannerisms (such as strokes nose or ear while speaking), nervous cough, habitually uses a particular phrase or phrases, peculiar walk (rolling, swinging slouching), speaks of some particular part of the world or country, rich relatives, experience, prowess at games; accomplishments (plays piano or other instrument, performs conjuring tricks or acrobatic feats), smokes (if a pipe, shape or make, gold or silver band, brand of tobacco; if cigarettes, brand, chain-smoker, makes own, peculiar manner of holding it); drinks beer, wine or spirits—favourite brand; associates with prostitutes; takes snuff.

M.P.-79-97820/1M C30

BUILD: As in item 7 on Chart.

FACE: Round, oval, long, wrinkled, flabby, fat, thin, high cheek-bones; expression—vacant, scowling, pleasant.

HAIR ON FACE: Beard (shape and colour), moustache (size, shape, colour, waxed), dark chin, sideburns.

FOREHEAD: As in item 6 on Chart.

EYES: Colour, cast, blind, missing, glass, red-rimmed, long lashes, wears spectacles (for reading, or habitually—horn-rimmed, pince-nez, bi-focal, shape of lens or frame), eyelid droops.

MOUTH: As in item 5 on Chart.

TEETH: Clean, discoloured, decayed, widely spaced, irregular, overlap, dentures, fillings, gaps, gold-crowned, toothless.

EARS: As in item 8 on Chart.

VOICE: Accent, gruff, melodious, high-pitched, deep, loud, soft, effeminate, affected, lisp, stammer, or other impediment, difficulty in pronouncing certain words or letters.

HAT or CAP: Colour and type.

TIE and SHIRT: Colours.

CLOTHING WORN: Colours and type.

SHOES: Colour and type.

ANY NAMES USED BETWEEN CRIMINALS.

PLACES FREQUENTED: Dance halls (good or low-class), greyhound race-tracks, steeplechase courses, flat-race courses, pony trotting courses, dirt-tracks, billiards saloons, type of public houses—any particular bar, class of hotel—using lounge or bar.

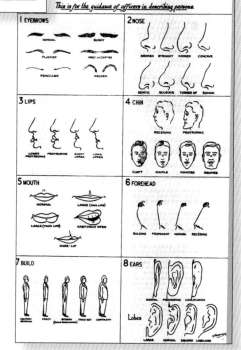

DESCRIPTIVE AID CHART
This is for the guidance of officers in describing persons.

POLICE PROCEDURES

What happens now...

There is a National Custody Record system that generates the necessary charge sheets and associated forms for completion, when a person is arrested. These forms are completed by the Custody Sergeant and the civilian custody staff whilst the offender is in custody.

This is a national computerised system and the forms are structured so that a consistency is brought to the descriptions being given. This assists when searching recorded descriptions in the investigation of crimes where a partial description may be given by a witness.

Acknowledging Senior Officers

I Remember When...

Memory of:
Charlie Phillips *(Joined Berkshire in 1951, retired in 1977 from Newbury).*

Charlie remembers that early in his service, while stationed at Windsor, the Superintendent in a monthly meeting informed all PCs that when on cycle patrol he expected them to acknowledge a senior officer, by doing a smart 'eyes right or left' as they passed them.

Shortly afterwards Charlie, while cycling around a roundabout, saw his Superintendent approaching from a side road riding his bicycle, apparently enroute home for his lunch. Charlie did as instructed and did a smart 'eyes left' while continuing to cycle around the roundabout.

It would appear that the Superintendent had not thought through his original instruction as he was unsure how to respond. Charlie saw the Superintendent trying to acknowledge Charlie's 'eyes left', start to wobble and then fall off his bicycle. However Charlie did not stop and continued around the roundabout as if he had not seen the Superintendent's embarrassment. Nothing was later mentioned about the incident.

POLICE PROCEDURES

What happens now...

The military-style recognition of senior officers is no longer required.

I Remember When...

Memory of:
Dick Allen *(Joined Berkshire as a boy clerk in 1948 at Newbury - later role changed to police cadet - following return from national service appointed as a constable in 1952, retired in 1984 from Banbury).*

Dick remembers that when the Berkshire Constabulary moved Headquarters to Sulhamstead it was only Inspectors and above who were permitted to enter through the front door of the White House. All other ranks had to use the back door.

What happens now...

Such restrictions are not applicable today.

POLICE PROCEDURES

The Beat System

Also see entries under POLICE DUTIES – Patrolling the Beat and POLICE TRAINING – Patrolling the Beat.

I Remember When...

Memory of:
Geoff Allen *(Joined Reading Borough as a police cadet in 1957, appointed as a constable in 1959, retired in 1985 from Ascot).*

Geoff remembers the beat system that existed in Reading when he joined and basically remained until the introduction of the Panda system in 1967.

The town was split into inner and outer beats. At one time there were a total of 25 beats, that was later extended to 42 beats covering the Borough. Geoff states that with the 25 beat system there was a constable on patrol on each beat 24 hours a day, seven days a week. Occasionally, to cover manpower shortages, a constable would be required to cover one-and-a-half beats or two beats for a shift. The 42 beat system was started when intermediate shifts were introduced. The shift system would then be the basic 0600-1400, 1400-2200 and 2200-0600, with intermediate shifts of 0800-1600 or 1000-1800 covering the day, and 1600-2400 and 1800-0200 covering the evening.

The beat system was based on police boxes and police pillars and, where these were not available, nominated telephone kiosks or other telephone points. The police boxes were large enough for a constable to go inside, and were normally equipped with a table, chair and toilet. *See entry under Communication – Conference Points.* There would be a light on top of the box which could be activated from the police station to summon the patrolling police constable. Police pillars were equipped with a telephone and, in some cases with a light, similar to the police box, that could be activated from the police station. Although it was hoped that the flashing light would alert the patrolling constable, often the light would first be seen by a member of the public who would draw the patrolling constable's attention to it.

Geoff remembers that the 'ring in' point in Broad Street, Reading was a wooden telephone box that was also shared with the Reading Borough bus inspectors.

POLICE PROCEDURES

It should be remembered that the beat system with police boxes, police pillars and conference points was designed to ensure that an area was patrolled and that there was a method of communication between the station and the patrolling constable. Car radios were not introduced until 1952 and personal radios were not introduced until 1965, which allowed the introduction of the Panda system – *see following entry.*

The inner beats paraded at the police station situated in Valpy Street, Reading. The outer beats paraded at police boxes situated around the outer wards of the Borough. The inner beats were patrolled on foot and the outer beats on pedal cycles, kept in the police box.

All officers had to parade 15 minutes prior to the start time of their shift, e.g. for a 2200-0600 duty the parade time was 2145. The additional 15 minutes was unpaid.

Geoff remembers that the parade at the Police Station, up until the introduction of the Panda system, was very much based on military lines. Up to 15 constables would line up with their truncheons in one hand and pocket book in the other. They were then called to attention and when an Inspector was present they had to refer to the Sergeant taking the parade as 'Sir'.

At the parade, constables were addressed by their number rather than their name. They were allocated the section and beat number they were to patrol, their meal break time and their ring-in time.

Geoff (PC 46 Allen) gives the following example "46, Beat 1 of the 1st. 15 minute rings, 1.30am meal".

Geoff remembers that although constables were allocated to beats at the parade, this was a confirmation that this would be the beat they would cover on that shift, as normally constables were allocated to a beat by the Chief Inspector (Patrol) and would remain allocated to the beat for up to nine weeks.

The 'ring-in' times were spaced out across an hour and it was a means of checking that the constable was on the beat and was accounted for. It also ensured that the station was able to contact a police officer at five minute intervals, should the need arise. The 'ring-in' was made from a police box or police pillar that was on the designated beat. Where no box or pillar existed, the officer stood at a designated telephone box, where the station would ring them.

At the conclusion of the parade, the constables marched out of the police station in single file, into Valpy Street and along to Blagrave Street and the Town Hall where they would separate to go to their designated beats.

POLICE PROCEDURES

The constable would then patrol their beat until their meal break time when, if they were an inner beat, they would return to the police station, or if an outer beat they would go to their police box. Meal breaks, which were initially 30 minutes, had to be taken as directed. No other refreshment breaks were allowed and if a constable was found having a cup of tea while on patrol, this was considered a disciplinary offence.

At the conclusion of the duty, the inner beats would return to the parade room at the police station (which would then have been vacated by the oncoming shift) where they would again line up and answer to their number when called, to ensure all were accounted for. They would then receive the order to 'Dismiss'.

Geoff remembers that each shift of constables in Reading were split into three sections. Each section would be under the supervision of a Sergeant and each section would be responsible for an area of the Borough. With the 25 beat system, two sections covered eight beats each, and one section covered nine beats. The sections were designated sections one, two and three.

Panda system in Reading

I Remember When…

Memories of:
Geoff Allen *(Joined Reading Borough as a police cadet in 1957, appointed as a constable in 1959, retired in 1985 from Ascot)*
Personal memory.

Geoff and I remember that the Panda system being introduced into Reading Borough in 1967. I lived on the outskirts of Reading and remember the article in the local paper with the picture of nine Vauxhall Viva panda cars lined up, each with a police constable, in Forbury Gardens, Reading. The Panda system was possible as the constables were always in contact through car radios and personal radio. The town had been split into nine areas, each would be patrolled by a constable in a panda car. The constables, while on patrol, were expected to leave their 'panda' at various locations and patrol on foot. Contact was available at all times through the personal radio system.

I remember that when I went to Reading in 1976 as a shift Inspector, that there were four patrol shifts, maintaining the 24 hour cover.

POLICE PROCEDURES

Each shift had eight panda beats to cover, plus five foot beats covering the town centre.

Each shift had selected constables who normally covered a nominated panda area. Four of the panda cars were based at the police boxes surrounding the town centre. This was a carry over from the old Reading Borough beat system. The outer boxes/pandas were based at Cemetery Junction, Whitley, Tilehurst and Caversham.

When the constables paraded at these individual boxes they were briefed by one of the shift sergeants over the telephone. The remaining constables paraded in the police station, although the military style parade had finished. Each panda was normally crewed by one police constable, even on the 2200-0600 night shift.

I remember that due to shift manpower levels it was not always possible to cover all of the panda areas and all of the town centre foot beats. I and the sergeants occasionally made decisions concerning which areas to merge for patrol purposes.

Pandas on Parade in Forbury Gardens, Reading

116

POLICE PROCEDURES

The panda system also incorporated Area Beat Officers (ABOs). Each panda area was split into two, occasionally three area beats. A constable was allocated to each area beat. They normally worked a shift system covering between 0800 and 2400, but they had some flexibility to adjust their shifts to meet the commitments on their beats. The idea was to leave the constable on their beats but, due to manpower shortages and other commitments, often constables had to assist in covering the pandas.

What happens now...

The beat system and panda system as outlined no longer exists. The 24 hour cover for a Local Police Area (LPA) is provided by the response shift, who are generally on mobile patrol. The role of the Area Beat Officer (ABO) has effectively been replaced by Community Teams, made up of police officers and police community support officers (PCSO).

Oxford City launches panda cars

POLICE PROCEDURES

Fuel for police vehicles

I Remember When...

Memory of:
Personal memory.

I remember that when I went to Woodley in 1965 and again when I was at Twyford in 1967, the procedure for getting petrol for the police vehicles was to fill the vehicles with petrol from two gallon petrol cans that were kept in a locked metal bin at Woodley Police Station.

When all the petrol cans in the store became empty, a constable had to load the empty cans into the rear of the police van, drive to Bracknell Police Station, and fill the cans up from the divisional petrol pump at Bracknell. When all cans were full, the van was driven back to Woodley and the cans placed in the petrol store. As a police cadet at Woodley, I assisted in this duty on several occasions.

Looking back now, I can see the logic and cost savings in the bulk purchase of petrol. I am not sure if the savings would still have been there, taking into account the time of the constable and the actual fuel cost of the petrol run.

When we amalgamated in 1968 into the Thames Valley Constabulary, the petrol store was replaced by an arrangement with the local garage at Woodley, where a petrol issue book was maintained.

What happens now...

Each police vehicle has a fuel card and this can be used at nominated petrol stations throughout the Force area.

POLICE PROCEDURES

Notice of Intended Prosecution

A Notice of Intended Prosecution (NIP) was required by the Road Traffic Act to be served (personally or by post) on a possible offender, within 14 days of the incident. The offences requiring an NIP were dangerous or careless driving, speeding, or failing to comply to traffic signals or signs.

The reason for an NIP was to draw the attention of the possible offender to the incident within a time that they should be able to recall the incident.

I Remember When...

Memories of:
Dick Godfrey *(Joined Buckinghamshire in 1956, retired in 1986 from Newbury).*
Personal memory.

Dick remembers that, in Buckinghamshire up until the early 1960s, a Notice of Intended Prosecution *(NIP)* had to be signed by the Superintendent. To get one sent, an officer had to first complete a report headed 'Application for NIP'. This was submitted to Divisional Administration to be approved by the Officer in Charge, who would then have the NIP typed and signed by the Superintendent. It was then returned to Divisional Administration who would send it off by recorded delivery as proof of receipt within 14 days was required.

    Dick remembers that following a suggestion made by him at a Divisional meeting, the system was changed allowing NIPs to be sent out at a local level. The change was approved after a trial of the new system took place on the Slough Division.

    I remember that the system had certainly changed when I was on Traffic at Taplow in 1972. I was the investigating officer into a multi-vehicle traffic accident on the M4 in which any one of eight drivers could have committed an offence of dangerous or careless driving. I personally typed and sent out eight NIPs. However the receipt of the NIP caused some of the drivers when I interviewed them to be somewhat hostile, complaining that they were the innocent victims of other drivers.

POLICE PROCEDURES

When the reasons for the NIP were explained, and after their account of their involvement, I was able to withdraw 5 at the time of interview, however the service of the NIPs within the required 14 days, enabled the prosecution of 3 drivers.

This memory will be common to many officers who will have their own memories of the difficulties sometimes encountered with the requirement for the NIP.

What happens now...

NIPs are still applicable for some offences today and the notice is within the various forms issued or sent out as a result of an offence being detected. NIPs are no longer required where a vehicle has been involved in a traffic accident.

PC and Panda Car

POLICE PROCEDURES

Parade for Duty

I Remember When...

Memories of:
Ken Amery *(Joined Berkshire as a police cadet in 1964, appointed as a constable in 1966, retired in 1996 from Windsor)*
Geoff Allen *(Joined Reading Borough as a police cadet in 1957, appointed as a constable in 1959, retired in 1985 from Ascot)*
Cameron Floate *(Joined Oxfordshire in 1951, retired in 1981 from Maidenhead)*
Rodney Watson *(Joined Berkshire as a police cadet in 1964, appointed as a constable in 1965, retired in 1995 from Taplow Traffic)*
Personal memory.

All can remember the requirement to parade 15 minutes prior to the start of a shift. Dependant upon the station the nature of the parade varied - some being very formal, based on military lines *(See entry under the Beat System).*

This 15 minutes was unpaid and, where you were responsible for taking the parade, the time preparing for the parade had to be added on, again unpaid. e.g. as a Shift Inspector in Reading for a 2200-0600 shift **I** arrived at 2130 to liaise with the Inspector going off duty and ensure that the Sergeants had all the necessary information for the 2145 parade.

What happens now...

At the start of a shift, all officers on the shift will attend a briefing that starts when the shift starts. There are no longer formal parades, and there is no requirement for the briefing to start 15 minutes prior to the start of the shift.

There is a requirement that officers attending the briefing must be ready to be deployed from the briefing, so they will have arrived prior to the start of the shift to get ready for the briefing.

POLICE PROCEDURES

Pedal Cycle Register

I Remember When...

Memory of:
John Chatterton-Ross *(Joined Thames Valley in 1987, retired in 2007 from Beaconsfield).*

John clearly remembers the first time he was told to go out with PC 49. Only when he asked "Who is PC49?" did he realise it was Pedal Cycle 49. All Force pedal cycles had serial numbers and had to be signed out in the Cycles Register so that the location of each pedal cycle issued to a police station could be traced.

Obtaining keys for areas on beats

I Remember When...

Memories of:
Cameron Floate *(Joined Oxfordshire in 1951, retired in 1981 from Maidenhead)*
Geoff Allen *(Joined Reading Borough as a police cadet in 1957, appointed as a constable in 1959, retired in 1985 from Ascot)*
Eddie Edwards *(Joined Reading Borough as a Police Cadet in 1957, appointed as a constable in 1958, retired in 1987 from Reading).*

Cameron remembers when at Witney between 1953 and 1955 that when he was on nights he obtained the key to the park gates of Blenheim Park in order that, as part of his patrol and to make the required conference points, he could cycle through the park.

Geoff remembers that on night duty on certain foot beats in Reading constables had to collect the keys to the gates to two arcades, so they could enter the arcades and check the property.

Eddie remembers that, when on night duty, on the beat covering Duke Street in Reading he had to collect the keys to the Prosecution Department Office. The Prosecution Department Office was in a building separate from the police station and the keys enabled a security check to be made. A book was kept in the office that had to be signed by the patrolling constable certifying the time of their visit(s).

POLICE PROCEDURES

Time checks

I Remember When...

Memory of:
Personal memory.

I can remember that when I started in 1963 in the Control Room of the Berkshire Headquarters, a time check occurred at 0800 each morning.

Prior to 0800, a member of the control room staff would phone the speaking clock and ensure that the clock in the control room was accurate. Just before 0800 each tie line to the five main stations of Windsor, Maidenhead, Bracknell, Newbury and Abingdon were called up and connected in what would now be called a 'conference call'. As the big hand of the clock approached the designated point, the control room operator would say to the person at the divisional station "The time is now 0800".

I am not sure what occurred at the divisional end, but it was obviously a procedure that stemmed from the days of inaccurate time pieces, but it was still continuing in 1963.

What happens now...

It seems hard to believe, in today's technological environment when time is automatically recorded on everything, that time checks were still required in 1963. However, that said, people are still late for duties and appointments!

POLICE TRAINING

Initial Training

I Remember When...

Memories of:
Jack Penny *(Joined Reading Borough in 1951, retired in 1983 from Reading Traffic)*
Personal memory.

Jack remembers that when he joined in 1951 his initial training took place in the District Police Training Centre at Sandgate, Kent and lasted three months.

I can remember that when I was appointed a constable in 1966 my initial training also took place at Sandgate. The course lasted 13 weeks and took place Monday to Saturday morning. There were two long weekends when we finished on the Friday. Each weekend we had to report back to the Training Centre by Sunday evening and were restricted to the Centre at all times, with the only evening out being Wednesdays.

Sandgate was the District Police Training Centre for the South East of England and took constables from Berkshire, Hampshire, Surrey, East and West Sussex, Kent, Reading Borough and Brighton Borough. There were approximately 60 constables on each intake, split into three classes, each under the supervision of a Sergeant. At any one time there were two intakes at the Centre, the junior intake just starting the first half of their training and the senior intake in the second half of their training.

Accommodation was in dormitories, and each morning the dormitory had to be cleaned and bedding folded into 'bed blocks'. Rooms were inspected by the Duty Sergeant. Following breakfast, all officers paraded on the Parade Ground, and you were then inspected by the Duty Inspector. It was very much military-based.

All constables on the initial training were split into duty squads. Duty squads were on duty from after the normal day time lessons and were allocated duties connected to the running and security of the Training Centre. On one occasion during the 13 weeks a squad would be the duty squad over a weekend which meant that they were unable to return home on that weekend.

Initial training, in addition to learning the laws and police powers, also covered first aid, self defence, life saving and drill. As part of the law learning, we had to learn up to 100 definitions relating to the law, which we were tested on weekly.

POLICE TRAINING

Many retired police officers can still remember some of the definitions. The first definition was

Constable

A citizen, locally appointed, but having authority under the crown for the:

- Protection of life and property
- Maintenance of order
- Prevention and detection of crime
- Prosecution of offenders against the peace.

Assessment tests covering the legislation taught doing the course, took place at regular intervals, with a final written examination on which your course report was based. We also had to pass a first aid examination and were expected to achieve a Bronze Medallion in life saving. I can remember that my life saving test took place in the open air seawater pool at Folkestone, in late October. We swam fast to keep warm!

I am aware that a similar training routine took place at Eynsham Hall, near Witney, for officers who joined Oxfordshire, Buckinghamshire, Bedfordshire, Hertfordshire, Norfolk, Suffolk, Cambridge and City of London, as in 1974 I completed the two week practical element of my Police Duties Instructors training course at Eynsham Hall.

All newly-joined police officers were on probation for two years. During my first two years, in addition to the 13-week initial course there was a two week intermediate probation course and a two week final probation course, both at District Police Training Centres.

In 1966 there were few practical exercises involved in the initial training (The main practical exercise involved dealing with a traffic accident). This was left to learning 'on the job'. There was no formal in-force induction or local procedure course, again learning was 'on the job'.

Although it appears that Initial Training had changed little over many years between when **Jack** joined and **I** joined, by 1974 when I became a Training Sergeant, an in-force one week induction course had been added to the start of the initial training, and an in-force two week local procedure added to the end of the course.

For more details of in-force training during the first two years of service see the next entry - Probationary Training.

POLICE TRAINING

By 1974, when I completed my Police Duty Instructor's course, the content of the initial training course had changed. Each theory lesson was structured around learning objectives, and the subjects taught during one week were assessed through an objective test at the start of the next week. In addition, linked to the learning objectives, more practical exercises had been added.

Probationary Training

I Remember When...

Memory of:
Personal memory.

All newly-joined police officers were on probation for two years. During my first two years (1966-1968), in addition to the 13-week initial course there was a two week intermediate probation course and a two week final probation course, both at District Police Training Centres.

Eynsham Hall - 1953 - Police initial training and practical traffic accident

POLICE TRAINING

In 1966 there were few practical exercises as part of the initial training, this being left to learning on the beat on completion of initial training. There was also no formal in-force induction, or local procedure course. After the initial course, the only formal training was the intermediate and final courses held back at the District Training Centres.

At the beginning of the 1970s, each Division within Thames Valley had a Training Sergeant. Between 1974 and 1976, **I** was the Training Sergeant on 'C' Division which covered Slough, Maidenhead, Windsor and Bracknell.

The initial training of constables had changed to objective based training and their was a training programme during their probation provided by the Divisional Training Sergeants. I had a structured syllabus that had to be followed on a fortnightly basis. Every probationary constable had to complete the syllabus. To do this they had to attend four hours of theory training every two weeks, over a period of about 16 months. Each training session covered a different subject under the three headings of criminal law, traffic law and law relating to general police duties.

'C' Division had approximately 80 constables on probation, of which between 50 and 60 had to attend the divisional training. As the Training Sergeant I scheduled five periods from 1400-1800 over a two-week period.

Assessment tests were held after every four training sessions and the results were included in the constable's intermediate and final probation reports.

What happens now...

The initial training and probationary training for new police officers has changed completely.

It is one of the changes to the police service not directly brought about by developing technology, but as a result of a review undertaken by Her Majesty's Inspectorate of Constabulary (HMIC) entitled 'Training Matters' which found that, in today's society, the training of police officers was not fit-for-purpose.

The initial training process is now referred to as 'Foundation Training'. There are no longer District Training Centres. All training is based at Force level, but on a national curriculum and with student officers working to achieve a Diploma in Policing by the end of their probation.

POLICE TRAINING

The change to Force-based training occurred in May 2006 with the introduction of the Initial Police Learning and Development Programme (IPLDP). The initial idea was for newly-appointed officers to travel on a daily basis to centres where the IPLDP courses were taking place. Within Thames Valley, centres were established at Reading University, Abingdon and Witney College in Abingdon and Aylesbury College. The training was provided by police officers but effectively the new police officers were students at the learning institutions, mixing with the other students. Initially they attended in plain clothes but this was later changed to attendance in uniform.

In 2011, IPLDP (now referred to as Foundation Training) returned to the Force Training Centre at Sulhamstead. Foundation Training is structured into four phases, and totals two years duration.

***Phase 1** takes place mainly in the potential officer's own time. Under a provisional offer of appointment they attend an Induction weekend (Weekend A) which is then followed by First Aid training on Weekend B. People who hold a recognised first aid qualification need not attend Weekend B. There then follows a period of pre-joining distance learning. Subject to satisfactory completion, the recruit will then receive a formal offer of appointment and the Phase ends with a one-week introduction during which the officers will be sworn in as constables.*

***Phase 2** is a one-week called 'Community Engagement'. The idea of this week is for the new officers to obtain an understanding of the various communities and minority groups that make up the Thames Valley population. It is personally structured dependant upon the background of the officer and will include various attachments to community centres, care homes, and local community organisations.*

***Phase 3** is under the overall supervision and monitoring of the Personal Development Unit (PDU), covering the Local Police Area (LPA) on which the officer is stationed. It is split between structured patrol activities with a tutor constable and learning based at the Force Training Centre. The last element of Phase 3 is a one week Preparation for Independent Patrol.*

***Phase 4,** covers 74 weeks and is under the heading of 'Independent Patrol'. During this period the new officer will attend a standard driving course, and attachments to their Neighbourhood Policing Team, plus a Crime attachment, before joining their shift on the Local Police Area (LPA).*

During the whole period they are under continuous assessment concerning their overall development as a police officer, which includes their levels of fitness.

POLICE TRAINING

It will be noticed that drill and formal parades are no longer part of the training process. Swimming and life saving to the level previously undertaken has also ceased. Officers are trained in the element of throwing a lifeline to a person in distress, and all police vehicles are being provided with the equipment.

The initial training of police officers is still under review and a two-year Foundation Degree in Policing, will shortly be available for potential officers to take at various universities around the Thames Valley. Whilst studying for their degree potential recruits will also work as Special Constables. Those who are successful in obtaining the Foundation Degree will, subject to passing the National Assessment Centre, be able to join at Phase 4 of the IPLDP.

People considering a career as a police officer are being encouraged to join first as a Police Community Support Officers (PCSO) or as a Special Constable.

Class of police persons

POLICE TRAINING

Divisional Training

I Remember When...

Memory of:
Personal memory.

I remember that when I became a Divisional Training Sergeant in 1974, the role included more than probationary training. I was also responsible for the divisional placement, supervision and divisional training of police cadets based on the division. This included arranging a weekly training day involving life saving, map reading and physical exercises, including some long distance walks - longer if the map reading failed!

In addition, the training sergeant was responsible for the training of special constables, as there was no Force-based training for special constables. Some training of traffic wardens and young people taking the police service as the community service section of their Duke Of Edinburgh Award was also involved.

When new legislation came in it was expected that the training sergeant would provide the necessary briefings across the division, and at one time I was also required to provide refresher and updated training to the police support units *(PSUs)* based on the division.

What happens now...

The whole structure of Divisional Training has changed. Each Local Policing Area (LPA) is covered by a Professional Development Unit (PDU). This unit, under the supervision of a Sergeant, is staffed by police constables and civilian trainers. It organises and arranges courses required by officers on the division and also provides Teams in Action training days for all officers on the LPAs.

POLICE TRAINING

Officers are assisted in identifying and establishing their training needs through the completion of the annual Professional Development Review (PDR) which has taken over from the annual appraisal. A PDR is an ongoing process, and all stages and updates are recorded on the computer system. Part of the assessment of line managers is the completion of PDRs by personnel that they line manage.

Driver Training

It is only right that police officers should have and maintain a high standard of driving. Listed below are memories about how this standard was assessed and the training that was given.

Initial authorisation

I Remember When...

Memory of:
Cameron Floate *(Joined Oxfordshire in 1951, retired in 1981 from Maidenhead).*

Cameron was for some years the rural beat officer covering the Wargrave Beat, part of the Twyford Section. Initially he covered the beat and all his travel requirements on bicycle *(See entry under Police Duties – Cycle Beats).*

Berkshire Constabulary started to issue Velocette motorcycles (commonly referred to as 'Noddy Bikes') to some rural beat officers, and one was issued to Cameron. The problem was that he was not a qualified motorcyclist.

To overcome this problem, the force did not send him on a course (possibly one did not exist) but issued him with a set of 'L' plates which he displayed on the 'Noddy Bike' as he patrolled his beat. 'L' plates continued to be displayed until he passsed his test. Cameron does admit that he was subject to some micky taking!

Oxfordshire Constabulary helmet plate

POLICE TRAINING

I Remember When…

Memory of:
Personal memory.

I remember my first day at Bracknell on return from Initial Training (1966). In the morning I, together with the two other constables from my initial training course, went to Sulhamstead to see the Chief Constable. In the afternoon, I paraded with the 1400-2200 shift at Bracknell, which was the shift I had been allocated to.

The Sergeant informed me that he had arranged a driving assessment for me at 1500, using the Bracknell Austin A.60 van, a column change vehicle. I had not driven a column change vehicle before so the Sergeant instructed another constable to take me out in the van, find a quiet road, and let me get used to it.

We returned to the Station at 1500 and I went out with the local Mobile Department Sergeant who, after approximately a 45-minutes assessment, informed me that I was authorised to drive police cars and vans, but not the large Austin one-tonne van, or the Austin 110 Mobile Department Patrol car, for which other assessments were required.

At 1615 I was assisting in the public enquiry office, waiting to go off duty at 1700 when a message to inform a relative of a death was received. The request, included the requirement for the message to be delivered as soon as possible.

The Sergeant assessed that there was no other constables available (all other officers were on patrol, with conference points and not immediately contactable). As I had passed my driving assessment I could drive the station van and therefore I could deliver the message. I had been a police cadet therefore knew the radio procedure and was told to make sure I booked on the radio with the Control Room. I was then shown on a map where I had to go and was sent out to deliver the death message on my own, on my first day of operational duty. This was certainly and example of 'on the job' training!

The radio operator in the Berkshire Control Room was not aware of my somewhat limited operational experience, only the fact that they now had a mobile unit in the Bracknell area which could be deployed to any commitment that came up.

I delivered the message and returned to the police station without another call.

Authorisation to drive specialist vehicles

I Remember When...

Memory of:
Personal memory.

I remember that my assessment to drive specialist types of vehicles went along similar lines to my assessment to drive a standard police vehicle. *(See above entry)*

The same Mobile Sergeant assessed and approved me to drive the large Austin one-ton van, and the Velocette motor cycle. I needed the authorisation to ride the Velocette for my posting, on marriage, to Twyford (1967).

Later in service a member of the driving school, after a short assessment test, assessed and approved me to drive the Force coach and the prison van. Both these assessments took place after I had been on traffic *– see following memory.*

What happens now...

The Force has a driving school based at Banbury, which is part of Learning and Development. Driving courses are offered and all drivers have to pass an assessment to drive at various levels. The first is the Standard Course, which takes three weeks. This enables a person to drive a police car, but not using the blue lights. A further assessment and course is required to be authorised as a response driver, and further assessments for standard driving of the larger personnel carriers and response driving of personnel carriers.

POLICE TRAINING

Assessment for Traffic Department and to drive Traffic Cars

I Remember When...

Memory of:
Personal memory.

I remember that in 1969 when I applied for Traffic Department, the first part of the application process was an assessment by the driving school constable as to my potential to drive a traffic car.

My application for traffic was successful (it appears it was all done on paper as I cannot remember having an interview) and I was posted to North East Traffic Area at Bletchley.

Here I was crewed with a First Class Advanced Driver (PC Tony Paddy). Initially I was not permitted to go out on my own. Tony's role, as part of my development as a traffic officer, was to advise me on my driving and correct any errors that he was detecting. As part of our duties we were performing M1 patrols in Jaguar 3.4 and Jaguar 4.2 XJ6 patrol cars. The patrols included enforcement of the 70mph speed limit - speeds in excess of 100mph were sometimes reached.

When Tony considered that I was safe to drive a traffic car on my own, an assessment test was arranged with the Aylesbury Driving School Sergeant, after which I was authorised to go on solo patrols.

At this time, the standard equipment on a traffic car to indicate that you were on an emergency call was one blue rotating light and a set of two tone horns.

After I had been on traffic for about four months, I attended my advanced driving course at Chelmsford. *(See following entry).*

First Class Advanced Driver Training

I Remember When...

Memories of:
John Harker *(Joined Oxfordshire as a police cadet in 1958, appointed as a constable in 1961, retired in 1987 from Police District Training Centre, Cwmbran)*
Personal memory.

John and I can both remember our Police Advanced Driver Training. We both attended Chelmsford, one of several regional centres in the country that ran the Advanced Driver training. Other traffic officers from Thames Valley and the constituent forces would have normally have attended Chelmsford or Maidstone. This often was the source of comments as to which of the driving schools was better.

The advanced course was four weeks long and the aim of all traffic patrol officers was to achieve a First Class Advanced mark. For both of us this was a hard course. For me it was my first driving course. You were under assessment for the full duration of the course, both by your instructor and another instructor who would, on at least one occasion during the week, swap roles with your instructor. This person was referred to as the 'check instructor'. Both instructors would assess and mark you on a weekly basis.

The course included a test against your knowledge of the Highway Code, an assessment test on the skid pan, and a driving assessment test of between one and one and a half hours with two other instructors. High marks had to be achieved in the weekly assessments, the theory, skid pan assessment and final drive. If any of the marks were below a certain level, a first class pass could not be awarded.

Both John and I have the same memory of driving home after the first week, thinking whether we were safe or competent to drive without our instructor sat by our side. This was the effect of the first week's training, where your confidence was reduced but built up in the following weeks.

Both of us achieved First Class Advanced passes.

POLICE TRAINING

What happens now...

The Force Driving School provides courses and assessment for pursuit driving and Advanced Driving. There are no longer any central Advanced Driving Centres, as all Advanced training is undertaken in-force.

Training for Patrolling the Beat

Details about what a beat was and what was expected when patrolling a beat are given in the sections – **Police Duties and Police Procedures,** *but what training was given to prepare officers for patrolling the beat?*

I Remember When...

Memory of:
Personal memory.

Following my initial police training (1966) **I** was posted to Bracknell. I remember that there was no structured training to link the theory learnt on the initial training course to the operational world of policing. On my first day at Bracknell I passed my authorisation to drive a police vehicle and was sent out, on my own, in the section van to deliver a death message. *(See previous entry under Driver Training – Initial authorisation).* On several shifts I went out with a more experienced constable, more to learn the area than how to patrol the beat, although some advice was given.

By 1974, when I trained as a Police Duties Instructor and the initial police training was based on objective training I believe that a 4 week attachment to a 'Tutor Constable' was in place. When a constable returned from initial training they were attached to a experienced constable for a 4 week period prior to going onto independent patrol. By 1983, when I was an Inspector on Training at Sulhamstead and responsible for Probationary Training, the Tutor Constable Attachment had been extended to 10 weeks, and all Tutor Constables undertook a 2 week training course.

POLICE TRAINING

What happens now...

Preparing a constable for patrolling a beat has changed. The old beat system has disappeared and how a constable patrols the area that they are allocated is left to their initiative, based on the training that they have received. The previous entry under Probationary Training outlines the initial training structure of police constables, and training for patrolling the beat is part of Phase 3 of the structure.

Other areas of training

Morse code and fire fighting

I Remember When...

Memory of:
Maurice Hedges *(Joined Berkshire as a junior clerk in 1940, appointed as a Constable in 1946, retired in 1975 from Wokingham).*

Maurice remembers that, as a junior clerk in 1940 in the Berkshire Headquarters he was trained in Morse code, should the use be necessary as a result of the war.

Maurice also remembers that in 1941, due to the possibility of incendiary bombs being dropped, all officers and civilians were trained in putting incendiaries out by using a stirrup pump. Pieces of an incendiary device were set alight in the centre of a yard and a person had to crawl along the ground with the end of the stirrup pump in one hand and aim the jet of water onto the incendiary. He states no person was exempt from the training, which was even completed by the Chief Constable.

POLICE TRAINING

What happens now...

Although Morse code is not used, the equivalent today would be training in the use of the various technologies that are used to communicate and carry out duties. Part of Learning and Development is IT Training, and another part is the Training Design team who develop e-learning courses to enable officers to use the various technical devices available today to access online learning.

Forensic Science

I Remember When...

Memories of:
John Abrams *(Joined Metropolitan Police 1953 in as a police cadet, appointed as a constable in 1956, joined Buckinghamshire in 1961, retired in 1987 from Headquarters, Traffic Management)*
Personal memory.

John remembers that in 1963 while on the Traffic Division of Buckinghamshire Constabulary, as part of the ongoing training as a traffic officer they visited the Forensic Science Laboratory at Aldermaston where they were introduced to some of the 'magic' of forensic science and how it could assist traffic officers in their role.

Shortly after the training, **John** was sent to a traffic accident where, on a dark road at night, a cyclist had been hit from behind by a motor car, the driver of which stated that the cyclist was not displaying lights. Remembering the 'magic' of forensic science, John took the rear light from the pedal cycle to the Forensic Science Laboratory where it was examined and they were able to confirm that the bulb had been alight when it was broken in the accident. The driver was convicted of careless driving.

I had a very similar incident in 1970, when on Traffic at Bletchley. I had received my briefing on the role of forensics and, when I attended an injury traffic accident involving a cyclist on the A5 at Great Brickhill, I was able to put it into effect. Similar situation to John, but on this occasion the Forensic Science Laboratory confirmed that the bulb was a 'cold break' and had not been on at the time of the accident, confirming the driver's version of the accident.

Police uniform

Listed below are some of the memories concerning police uniform.

I Remember When…

Memories of:
Geoff Allen *(Joined Reading Borough as a police cadet in 1957, appointed as a constable in 1959, retired in 1985 from Ascot)*
John Harker *(Joined Oxfordshire as a police cadet in 1958, appointed as a constable in 1961, retired in 1987 from Police District Training Centre, Cwmbran)*
Ken Amery *(Joined Berkshire as a police cadet in 1964, appointed as a constable in 1966, retired in 1996 from Windsor)*
Jamie Eves *(Joined Berkshire as a police cadet in 1965, appointed as a constable in 1966, retired in 1997 from Taplow Traffic)*
Personal memory.

Geoff remembers that when he first joined Reading Borough, constables during the winter on night duty were allowed to wear a closed neck tunic if they had retained one, after the change was made to open neck tunics with collars and ties.

Geoff also remembers that Reading Borough did not issue constables with handcuffs, which did cause problems – see his entry under *Police Duties – Patrolling the Beat.*

John as well as many others remember that until the 1970s they were issued with collar detached shirts. I believe the ratio was one shirt and six collars. With these shirts was the need for front and back studs, used to attach the collar to the shirt. These could easily be lost or mislaid, so most people had more than one set. A change of collar meant that a daily change of shirt was not always necessary, which made life somewhat easier for single officers.

POLICE UNIFORM

John and all of us remember the requirement that all officers should look the same when in uniform. Therefore if the decision was made to wear great coats on nights, all should wear great coats. The main example related to shirt sleeve orders, where approval had to be granted by a senior officer before tunics could be removed.

It was not until the very hot summers of the 1990s that approval was given for ties to be removed. By this time, issued ties had changed from the normal-style tie to the clip-on tie, that could be easily removed. The change had been brought about when health and safety became a requirement, and a normal tie could be used to strangle an officer if they were involved in a fight, whereas the clip-on tie just came off!

Jamie and I both remember that in Berkshire we were issued with two helmets and one flat cap. Helmets had to be worn when on foot or cycle patrol, and the flat cap when driving.

Two helmets were issued, as one had a chrome helmet plate which was for use during daylight hours and on the other the helmet plate was painted black, and was used on night duty. This was in line with the basic patrol concept that during the day you should be visible, for example walking down the outside of pavements, and at night be invisible by keeping to the shadows and walking down the inside of pavements. The black plate on the night helmet assisted with this.

When the panda car system was first introduced, the idea was that the vehicle should be used both for patrol and for transport to points where the car could be parked and time spent on foot patrol. It was therefore necessary to take both a flat cap for use when driving, and a helmet for use when walking.

I, as well as all officers, will remember that in addition to the tunic and trousers, the normal issue of uniform included a great coat for cold nights, a rain coat for rainy days, and a cape, for wearing when cycling, although it should be said some officers also used the cape when walking on cold nights. In addition we were all issued with handcuffs (except Reading Borough officers), truncheon and a whistle on a chain.

The whistle and chain will always be remembered as a distinctive part of the uniform. It was part of the uniform when the role of a police constable was first conceived, for use as a means of summoning assistance.

Berkshire PC ready for cycle patrol duty during the war

SPECIALIST SUPPORT UNITS

Armed Response Vehicles

In the past there were few specialist support units. There was uniform policing, mobile (later to become traffic) and CID. The first women police departments were developed in 1940s but it was not until the Sex Discrimination Act 1975 that women officers became fully integrated into the police force. The mounted section of the Thames Valley Police was formed in 1985, although many of the forces that formed the Thames Valley Constabulary in 1968 had previously had mounted sections. These had ceased to exist as the motor car developed as a form of transport.

Listed below is another memory linking past and present.

I Remember When...

Memory of:
Maurice Hedges *(Joined Berkshire as a junior clerk in 1940, appointed as a constable in 1946, retired in 1975 from Wokingham).*

Maurice remembers that in the early part of the Second World War (1939-1945) the Chief Constable of Berkshire introduced the forerunner of the now Armed Response Vehicle *(ARV)*. He decreed that the green Alvis car that the Force had would be manned by a police constable, who was his chauffeur, with a sergeant armed with an automatic weapon sat in the front seat, and two constables armed with rifles sat in the rear seat. The vehicle would then be available to respond to any report of Germans invading the country.

What happens now...

The Thames Valley Police have specially-trained firearms officers, and also specially equipped Armed Response Vehicles (ARVs). A 24 hour cover is provided across the Force by ARVs.

Terminology

Over the years terminology used within the police force has changed, as it has in many services and industries. Some examples are given below.

I Remember When...

Police officers **paraded** *for duty.*

We now attend a **briefing.**

I Remember When...

A police force was divided into **Divisions, Sub Divisions, Sectors and Beats.**

They were called Basic Command Units (BCUs), but the name has recently been changed to **Local Policing Areas (LPAs).**

TERMINOLOGY

I Remember When...

There was a **Traffic Department.**

This is now referred to as **Roads Policing.**

I Remember When...

There was a **Training Department.**

This is now referred to as **Learning and Development** *and each LPA is covered by a* **Professional Development Unit (PDU).**

TERMINOLOGY

I Remember When...

When we had **annual appraisals,** *well sometimes!*

This is now referred to as a **Personal Development Review (PDR).**

Thames Valley Police Roads Policing officer and car

"I REMEMBER WHEN…"   2ND EDITION.

I hope that you have enjoyed reading this edition of "I Remember When…"

If you have served in Thames Valley Police, or any of the constituent forces, it may have brought back some memories to you either on the subjects included or on other subjects that have not been included in this edition. If you have memories about policies, procedures or processes that were present during your service and feel they could be included in a 2nd edition of "I Remember When…", please forward them to me, and if sufficient memories are received I will author a second edition. The orginator of each memory used will receive a free copy of "I Remember When …" 2nd edition.

All proceeds from the sale of "I Remember When…" 2nd Edition, will be donated to the Police Rehabilitation Trust and Flint House.

To assist me in including your memories please complete the following proforma and send it to me at:

Tony Keep
43 Glendevon Road
Woodley
Reading
Berks
RG5 4PL

or if you have also joined the technological age of the computer, please contact me at tonykeep@btinternet.com

    Should you be a police officer who has served in another force and feel that a similar book could be made about memories from your force, I would be happy to advise anyone wishing to produce such a book, but only on the condition that monies raised go to The Police Rehabilitation Trust, Flint House or a similar charity.

Anthony R. Keep (Tony)

MEMORIES

"I Remember When..."

Name: ....

Address ....

Tel. No. .... EMail: ....

Force joined: .... Year:..

If a Police Cadet, year appointed as a Constable: ....

Year Leaving* / Retired*: .... Last Place Served: ....

* Please delete one

Memory:..

....

....

....

Approximate year(s) above occurred...

If more memories, please continue overleaf.

Send to:

Tony Keep
43 Glendevon Road
Woodley
Reading
Berks
RG5 4PL

Or email tonykeep@btinternet.com

Thank you